Options for Equality
in State Pension Age

Presented to Parliament
by the Secretary of State for Social Security
by Command of Her Majesty
December 1991

Cm 1723   LONDON: HMSO   £9.80 net

FOREWORD BY THE SECRETARY OF STATE FOR SOCIAL SECURITY

Since taking office, this Government has been committed to the protection and enhancement of the incomes of pensioners. We have also introduced a number of measures to increase choice and flexibility in pension provision. I announced in the House of Commons in June that we were now ready to address the next priority – establishing equality of treatment for men and women, and, in particular, tackling the issue of unequal pension ages in the state pension schemes.

This is a complex issue with implications for many people. I do not believe that it would be right for the Government to reach decisions on how equality should be achieved without wide public discussion. This paper has therefore been prepared to set out relevant information on the issues to help inform the debate.

There has already been great public interest in this important matter. I look forward to the debate that will take place over the next few months, which will help us to develop proposals for the future of state pension age.

TONY NEWTON

1. INTRODUCTION

1.1 Since 1940, when the state pension age for women was lowered from 65 to 60, much has changed. Not all men start work at 16 and keep working until they are 65. It is no longer the case that most women spend most of their working lives at home. There are more one-parent families and more second marriages. There has been substantial growth in occupational pensions coverage, personal savings and property ownership. Retirement decisions have therefore become both more complicated and more flexible.

1.2 The state retirement pension is now only one of many possible sources of income for people who are retired or approaching their retirement. Perhaps as a consequence, there is an increasing tendency for people to retire at an age other than that from which they are first entitled to their state retirement pension. A direct link between state pension age and the age at which an individual chooses to retire cannot necessarily be assumed. *(See Chapter 2, paragraphs 2.16 - 2.20 and Chapter 4, paragraphs 4.14 - 4.16.)*

1.3 Two recent changes to the law have increased an individual's choice of retirement age:

- the Sex Discrimination Act 1986 amended the Sex Discrimination Act 1975 to make it unlawful for an employer to have different retirement ages for men and women; and

- since 1 October 1989, payment of a retirement pension is no longer dependent on retirement from employment. Thus a person may now continue working past the pensionable age and receive a state retirement pension which will not be affected by the amount of earnings received.

Moving to the future

1.4 There are several respects in which the present social security system in the UK treats men and women differently, but the difference in state pension age - 60 for women and 65 for men - is the most fundamental. The Government is committed to removing that difference. The question is not whether it does so but how and when.

1.5 Changing the state pension age is of concern to most people of working age. When decisions have been taken, and the necessary legislation passed by Parliament, men or women or both may need to adjust their retirement plans to take account of a new state pension age. Alternatively people may find that, from some point in the future, the amount of state pension they can receive depends on when they first claim it.

1.6 There will be a range of financial effects as individuals, employers, insurance and investment companies, and the pensions industry adjust to the changes in state pension age and as these adjustments work their way through the economy. Changing state pension age will have important and complex implications both for millions of individuals of working age and for the economy of the UK. The Government will need to consider, and include in its proposals for legislation, a number of consequential changes for both state and occupational pensions and for other social security benefits.

1.7 Any consideration of changes to the state pension age must take into account a number of broad social and economic factors, such as:

- **trends in pensioners' incomes:** including the role that the state pension plays in pensioners' income *(see Chapter 3)*;

- **demography:** because the state scheme is a *'pay-as-you-go'* scheme, the expected relationship between the number of pensioners and the size of the workforce in the future is a very important factor *(see Chapter 4, paragraphs 4.1 - 4.13)*;

- **life expectancy:** *(see Chapter 4, paragraphs 4.17 and 4.18)*; and

- **spending on state retirement pension:** how much the current system is projected to cost both in absolute terms and as a percentage of the UK's gross domestic product (GDP) *(see Chapter 4, paragraphs 4.19 - 4.21)*.

1.8 The Government would welcome comments and views on two main questions:

- Is a common pension age approach to be preferred, and, if so, which age should be adopted and over what period should the change be implemented *(Chapter 6)*?

  or

- If a flexible pension age is preferred, which model should be adopted as the basis for preparing a detailed scheme *(Chapter 7)*?

The Government intends public discussion of these questions to extend to Northern Ireland as well as to Great Britain because of the principle of parity in social security provision throughout the UK. All figures quoted, however, relate to Great Britain only, for ease of comparison with other published material.

2. SOCIAL SECURITY AND RETIREMENT PENSION

Development of National Insurance and Retirement Pension

2.1 Old age pensions were first introduced in 1908, as means-tested pensions for men and women aged over 70. Contributory pensions were first introduced in 1925, funded from contributions from the employer, employee and the state: the 1925 scheme provided for flat rate payments for all pensioners over the age of 65, and for widows.

2.2 In 1940 women's pension age was lowered to 60 by the Old Age and Widows' Pensions Act. The new inequality was a response to a campaign by unmarried women in the 1930s, many of whom cared for dependent relatives for much of their lives. It also recognised the fact that, on average, married women were several years younger than their husbands.

2.3 The National Insurance Act 1946 provided for pensions funded by flat rate contributions. Funding problems arose when it was decided to pay full pensions immediately rather than linking the level of payments to the level of contributions. Growing numbers of older people in the 1950s and 1960s, together with increased benefit levels, compounded the problem and meant that flat rate contributions became unsustainable. The National Insurance Act 1959 was the first step towards relating the amount of national insurance contributions payable to the level of earnings and providing an earnings-related element in benefits. Since then the National Insurance Fund has continued to operate on a pay-as-you-go basis, with contributions in any one year funding benefit payments in that year. Graduated pensions, and the associated separate earnings-related contributions, were introduced in 1961 to provide benefits which supplemented the basic state retirement pension.

2.4 The 1959 Act also introduced 'contracting-out'. An employer could contract his employees out of the graduated pensions scheme if an occupational scheme provided its members with pension benefits at least equal to their graduated pension. (These were known as Equivalent Pension Benefits.) The graduated pension scheme was wound up in 1975, although accrued rights were retained.

2.5 In 1978 the State Earnings Related Pension Scheme (SERPS) was introduced. This added a new earnings-related pension, based on contributions from April 1978, to the flat rate basic pension. An employer could contract his employees out of SERPS, if the pension benefits provided by his occupational scheme were at least equivalent to SERPS. These equivalent benefits are known as Guaranteed Minimum Pensions (GMPs).

2.6 The Social Security Act 1986 introduced two main changes to SERPS for people reaching pension age after 1999. These were, firstly, to calculate entitlement to SERPS over the whole working life (i.e. 44 years for women, 49 years for men) rather than over the best 20 years of earnings; and, secondly, to reduce entitlement from 25% to 20% of the individual's average earnings between the upper and lower earnings limit. At the same time, it extended individuals' rights by allowing them to contract out of SERPS to join a personal pension scheme or to participate in a contracted-out *money purchase scheme*.

The Present System

Contributions

2.7 Employed people earning above a minimum weekly amount have to pay primary Class 1 contributions, and their employers have to pay secondary Class 1 contributions. These are used to fund a range of benefits on the pay-as-you-go basis *(see paragraph 2.3)*. The point at which an employee's earnings become liable for contributions is known as the lower earnings limit (LEL). At present the lower earnings limit is set at £52 per week. An employee who has earnings at or above the lower earnings limit will pay contributions on all earnings up to the level of the upper earnings limit (UEL), which is currently £390 per week. Class 1 national insurance contributions are based broadly on a percentage rate of earnings. The rate is lower for employees and employers who have contracted out of SERPS. Self employed earners are liable to pay Class 2 national insurance contributions on any level of earnings unless they have been granted exception from this liability on the grounds that their earnings fall below a certain level. Liability to pay primary Class 1 national insurance contributions (i.e. the employee's contributions) ceases once a person reaches pensionable age. However, the employer must continue to pay secondary Class 1 contributions if the employee continues in work.

Retirement Pension

2.8 The Social Security Act 1975 provides for 4 categories of Retirement Pension:

Contributory Pensions

1. Category A Retirement Pension - based on a pensioner's own contributions.

2. Category B Retirement Pension - based on a spouse's contributions.

Non-Contributory Pensions

> **3.**   Category C Retirement Pension.

> **4.**   Category D Retirement Pension.

Category A Retirement Pension

2.9   Category A pension may consist of both basic pension and SERPS *(see paragraph 2.14)*. If an individual has earned more than the specified lower earnings limit and has paid or been credited with sufficient contributions for the required number of years, he or she will qualify for a basic pension. However, for each of the requisite number of years for which sufficient contributions are not paid or credited the basic pension is reduced. No basic pension is paid if entitlement falls below 25%. It is possible within specified time limits to make good any gaps in contributions for previous years by payment of voluntary (Class 3) contributions.

2.10   For the purposes of national insurance contribution calculations, a person's working life usually starts at the beginning of the tax year in which age 16 is reached and ends with the tax year before the one in which pensionable age is reached: 65 for men and 60 for women. To qualify for a full basic pension a person must have paid contributions for about $^9/_{10}$ths of their working life, i.e. for 44 years for men and for 39 years for women. If a person cannot work because of 'home responsibilities', such as looking after a dependant, the number of contribution years required is in certain circumstances reduced. (Home Responsibilities Protection.)

Category B Retirement Pension

2.11   Category B pension can be paid to a wife or to a surviving spouse. When paid to a wife, it is a basic pension and the requirements are that both husband and wife have reached pension age, that the husband has taken his category A pension, and that the wife has either no category A basic pension entitlement or only a reduced entitlement. If she has category A basic pension entitlement at less than the rate of her category B, it is topped up to the level of category B and paid as a composite pension. Category B is also paid to a widow, and in certain circumstances a widower, over state pension age. When paid to a surviving spouse, the pension may consist of both basic pension and SERPS. *(See paragraph 2.14.)*

Category C Retirement Pension

2.12 Category C pension is a standard rate non-contributory retirement pension subject to a residence test and paid to people who were over pension age on 5 July 1948 and the wives and widows of such pensioners.

Category D Retirement Pension

2.13 Category D pension is a standard rate non-contributory retirement pension paid to people aged 80 and over who satisfy the residence condition and do not have a contributory pension, or whose contributory pension is less than the rate of category D.

SERPS

2.14 SERPS is the additional earnings-related pension scheme which has been in place since 1978 *(see paragraph 2.5)*. It is built up by paying Class 1 (employed earners') national insurance contributions. It is calculated as a specified percentage of earnings on which national insurance contributions have been paid since April 1978, revalued at pension age to take into account the increase in average earnings over that period. It is normally paid as an addition to the category A basic pension (or category B where appropriate - *see paragraph 2.11*). It can be paid on its own if there is no basic pension entitlement. As explained in *paragraph 2.5* it is possible to contract out of SERPS.

Supplements to Retirement Pension

2.15 An increase of retirement pension can be paid for dependants provided the relevant qualifying conditions are met. For pensioners with little or no other source of income and less than £8,000 savings, retirement pension may be supplemented by income support.

Pension Age and Retirement Age

2.16 Pension age and retirement age are not necessarily the same. Although the state retirement pension cannot be paid before state pension age, men who retire between the ages of 60 and 65 may claim income support without having to make themselves available for work. If entitled, they will have the basic *'pensioner premium'* of £13.75 included. The result of this is that a single man of 60 with savings of £3,000 or less and no earnings or other income will be entitled, at 1991 rates, to a weekly level of income support at least £1.40 in excess of the rate of basic retirement pension.

2.17 Invalidity pension is, broadly speaking, paid to those who have been incapable of work for 28 weeks, and follows their entitlement to sickness benefit. It can be paid until age 70 for men and age 65 for women. Claimants over pension age are paid at the same rate as the retirement pension to which they would otherwise have been entitled. Invalidity pension is not taxable whereas retirement pension does count as taxable income. The number of invalidity pensioners is increasing over time. Many of those receiving the benefit in the few years prior to pension age may in practice consider themselves to be retired.

2.18 Unlike invalidity pension, sickness benefit is paid at 5% less than the retirement pension rate at state pension age. It can however also be claimed, or continue to be received, for a period of 5 years after pensionable age, i.e. up to 65 for a woman and 70 for a man. Any entitlement to unemployment benefit will be paid at the retirement pension rate for anyone past state pension age.

Retirement after State Pension Age

2.19 There is nothing to stop people from continuing to work after state pension age if they wish to do so. Since the earnings rule and retirement condition were abolished in October 1989, anyone can claim their pension without reduction and remain in work. Such evidence as there is suggests that this change has not made a significant difference to the numbers who continue working.

2.20 Alternatively, people in work may defer taking their pension for up to five years and receive a higher pension when they do claim. Each year's deferral gives an extra 7.5%, approximately, of the rate of pension foregone. These additions are called increments.

3. OTHER SOURCES OF INCOME

Recent Trends in Pensioners' Incomes

3.1   Between 1979 and 1988, pensioners' net average income grew by 34% in real terms (an average of 3.3% each year).[1] It is clear that the main driving forces behind this increase were income from savings and occupational pensions. There was also a change in the composition of income.

3.2   In 1979 62% of pensioners had savings income. This had increased to 74% by 1988, when 78% of recently retired pensioners had income from some form of savings. Gross income from savings grew by 110%. This increase reflects both an increase in the volume of savings and an improvement in the real rate of return on investments. In addition, the trend towards wider property ownership should increase the value of pensioners' assets in years to come.

3.3   In 1979 41% of pensioners had income from occupational pensions. This had increased to 51% by 1988, when 62% of recently retired pensioners had such income. This trend is expected to continue, albeit at a slower rate, to at least the end of the century. Average gross income from occupational pensions grew by 99% in real terms in the period between 1978 and 1988.

3.4   The proportion of income from social security benefits has decreased from 61% in 1979 to around 51% in 1988, although income from all social security benefits grew by 14% . Over the coming decades, SERPS will form an increasingly important element of pensioner incomes and there may also be a reduction in the number of pensioners in receipt of income support.

3.5   Finally, pensioner earnings declined by about 6% over the period. In 1979 the proportion of income from earnings was 12%, which decreased to 8% by 1988. This seems to reflect the general trend for earlier retirement from paid employment. *Figure 1* shows the difference in the composition of pensioners' incomes in 1979 and 1988.

---

[1] Data on the incomes of pensioners in this chapter are derived from the Family Expenditure Survey (FES) 1988 and are based on pensioner units (i.e. either a pensioner couple or a single pensioner) rather than individual pensioners.

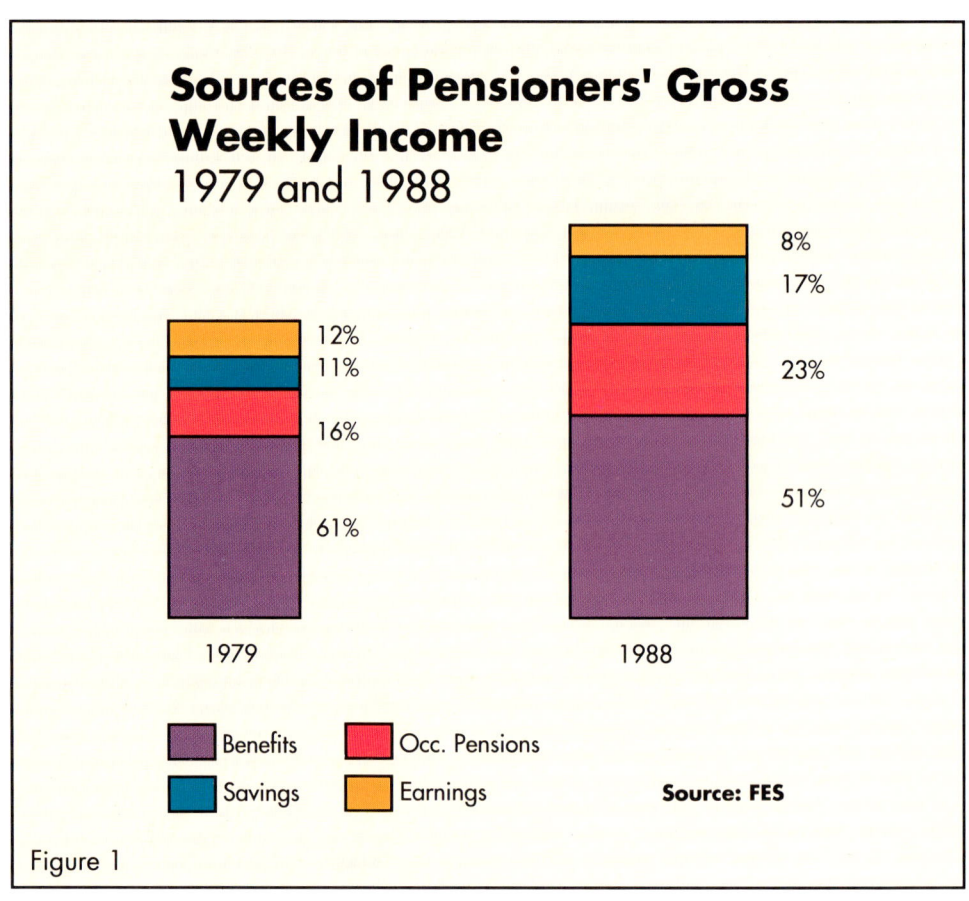

Sources of Pensioners' Gross Weekly Income
1979 and 1988

1979:
- 12%
- 11%
- 16%
- 61%

1988:
- 8%
- 17%
- 23%
- 51%

Benefits | Occ. Pensions
Savings | Earnings | **Source: FES**

Figure 1

Occupational and Personal Pensions

3.6 There are currently around 460,000 occupational pensions schemes with a membership of around 11 million people. Occupational pensions have become an increasingly important part of pension provision in the UK. In addition, pension funds are an important source of funds for the capital market. It is estimated that their current market value is around £320 billion.

3.7 The major form of private pension provision in the UK is through occupational pension schemes which are approved for contracting-out of SERPS.

3.8 Once a pension scheme is so approved, it becomes responsible for providing a pension in place of the additional pension provided through SERPS. In return, both the employer and employee pay national insurance contributions at a rebated rate. The level of the rebate is set to reflect the cost to the scheme of funding replacements for SERPS. *(See Chapter 2, paragraph 2.7.)*

3.9 Since the occupational scheme provides a replacement for SERPS the contracting-out conditions are based around the unequal state pension age.

4. THE BACKGROUND TO CHANGE

Demography

Number of pensioners

4.1   The group of people who will be above current state pension ages in the first half of the next century consists of women born before 1990 and men born before 1985. Unless there is a major change in net migration patterns or in current trends towards greater longevity, it is possible to forecast the size of this group with some confidence. The projected number of pensioners in Great Britain according to the Government Actuary's principal projections is shown in *Figure 2*[1].

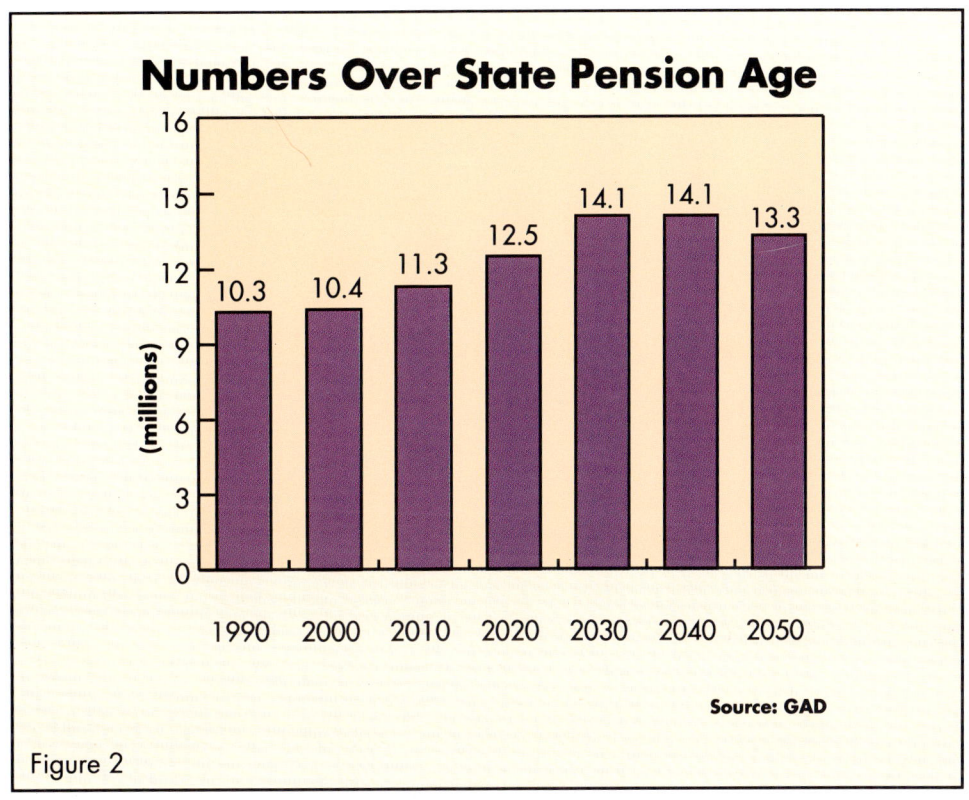

Numbers Over State Pension Age

Figure 2

4.2   There will be a significant increase in the number of people over state pension age - from 10.3 million in 1990 to a projected 13.3 million in 2050, peaking at 14.4 million in 2034 on the Government Actuary's principal projections, or at over 13 million on more pessimistic assumptions about longevity.

4.3   The peak in the numbers of pensioners is caused by the ageing of the people born during the 1960's *'baby boom'*. This will lead to a corresponding increase in the numbers reaching state pension age in the third and fourth decades of the next century.

---

[1] The Government Actuary's principal projections are the main population projections for Great Britain. The 1989 based National Population Projections prepared by the Government Actuary (OPCS Series PP2 No17) also set out variant projections assuming different fertility or mortality rates.

Proportion of Pensioners in the Population

4.4 Projections of the proportion of pensioners in the total population over the first half of the next century are inevitably more uncertain, as they require assumptions about future trends in the birth rate. Until recently, the birth rate had been falling in virtually all industrialised countries. In Britain, the generation born in 1940 had an average completed family size of 2.4 children, but it seems likely that women born in 1955 will, on average, have 2.0 children.

4.5 There are, however, signs that the downward trend in average completed family size is now ceasing. The Government Actuary's principal projections assume that the average will be 2.0 children for the generation now reaching childbearing age. However, scenarios can be envisaged with birth rates ten per cent more or less than this, causing (in the absence of substantial net migration) a working population ten per cent or so larger or smaller by the middle of the 21st century than in the projections used for the estimates in this paper. (*Chapter 5* gives some comparative international figures.)

4.6 *Table 1* and *Figure 3* set out the Government Actuary's principal projections for the total population, broken down into three age groups: children (ages 0-15), people of working age (ages 16-59 for women and 16-64 for men) and people over state pension age.

Table1: Population Projections 1991-2050 (Great Britain, Millions)				
	1990	**2010**	**2030**	**2050**
Under 16	**11.2**	**11.8**	**11.8**	**11.2**
Working age	**34.4**	**35.3**	**33.6**	**33.6**
Over state pension age	**10.3**	**11.3**	**14.1**	**13.3**
Total	**55.8**	**58.4**	**59.5**	**58.1**

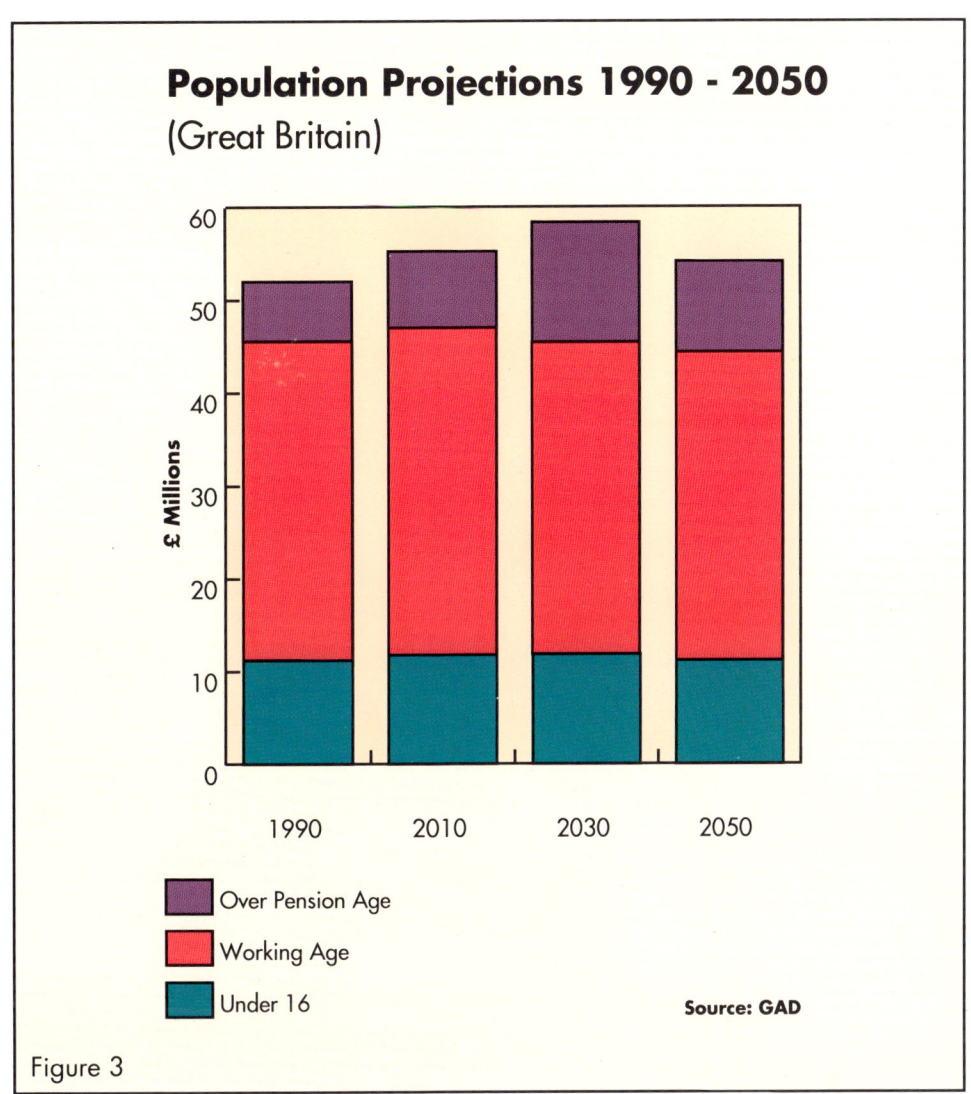

Population Projections 1990 - 2050
(Great Britain)

£ Millions

Legend:
- Over Pension Age
- Working Age
- Under 16

Source: GAD

Figure 3

4.7 *Table 1* and *Figure 3* show that at the same time as the number of pensioners increases next century, the population of working age is expected to fall , from 34.4 million in 1990 to 33.6 million in 2050. The ratio of these two numbers - the number of people of working age per pensioner - is an indicator of the capacity of the economy to provide for those adults no longer working. For this reason it is termed the *'support ratio'*. *Table 2* sets out projections of this ratio over the period 1990-2050.

Table 2: Number of people of working age per pensioner: the support ratio				
	1990	**2010**	**2030**	**2050**
People of working age per pensioner	3.4	3.1	2.4	2.6
Index 1990 = 100	100	91	71	76

4.8   Between 1990 and 2050, the support ratio is expected to decline from 3.4 to 2.6, reaching a low point of 2.4 in 2030. This fall of 24% from 1990 to 2050 suggests that the capacity of the economy to support its much larger pensioner population will come under considerable pressure. Even if the assumptions about mortality and fertility rates on which these figures are based are not borne out in practice, it seems likely that the support ratio will fall below 3.0. At worst, it could fall further below 2.5.

4.9   Table 3 shows how the support ratios would change if state pension age were equalised at age 60 and age 65.

Table 3: Support ratios for state pension ages of 60 and 65			
	2010	**2030**	**2050**
Age 60	2.6	2.0	2.2
Index *	76	59	65
Age 65	4.0	3.0	3.1
Index *	118	88	91

*1990 support ratio of 3.4 = 100 (see table 2)

4.10   The ratios in Tables 2 and 3 do not allow for the fact that some people of working age are not economically active, while some people over state pension age remain active. This could be important because it is upon those who are economically active that the cost of social provision will fall.

4.11 The number of adult dependants, as measured by those economically inactive aged 16 and over, is projected to rise by some 18% between 1990 and 2050. This is markedly less than the corresponding rise in the number of pensioners at 28%. *Table 3* sets out details of the movement over the period 1990-2050 in a variation on the support ratio that takes account of economic activity. This is the ratio of the number of economically active adults to the number of inactive adults in the population. This ratio depends on activity rate projections which are subject to some uncertainty. *(See Appendix 1, paragraphs 42-48.)*

Table 4: Economically active ratio				
	1990	**2010**	**2030**	**2050**
Active adults per inactive adult	**1.8**	**1.7**	**1.4**	**1.5**
Index 1990 = 100	**100**	**94**	**78**	**83**

4.12 The deterioration in this ratio from 1990 to 2050 of 17% is somewhat less marked than that of 24% in the support ratio. *Table 5* shows how these ratios would change if state pension age were equalised at age 60 and age 65. The impact on dependency of moving to common state pension ages of 60 and 65 measured in this way is less than with the support ratios shown in *Table 3*, although this depends on the assumption that retirement patterns are not primarily determined by state pension age.

Table 5: Economically active ratios for state pension ages of 60 and 65			
	2010	**2030**	**2050**
Age 60	**1.6**	**1.4**	**1.5**
Index *	**89**	**78**	**83**
Age 65	**1.8**	**1.5**	**1.6**
Index *	**100**	**83**	**89**

*1990 ratio of 1.8 = 100 (see table 4)

4.13 Neither the support ratio nor the economically active ratio is a perfect measure of dependency because neither takes account of variations in the cost to society imposed by different members of the same age group or different members of those economically inactive. For example, a person above state pension age who has retired on a substantial occupational pension will be counted as a dependant whilst a person on income-related benefits below state pension age will be counted as a non-dependant.

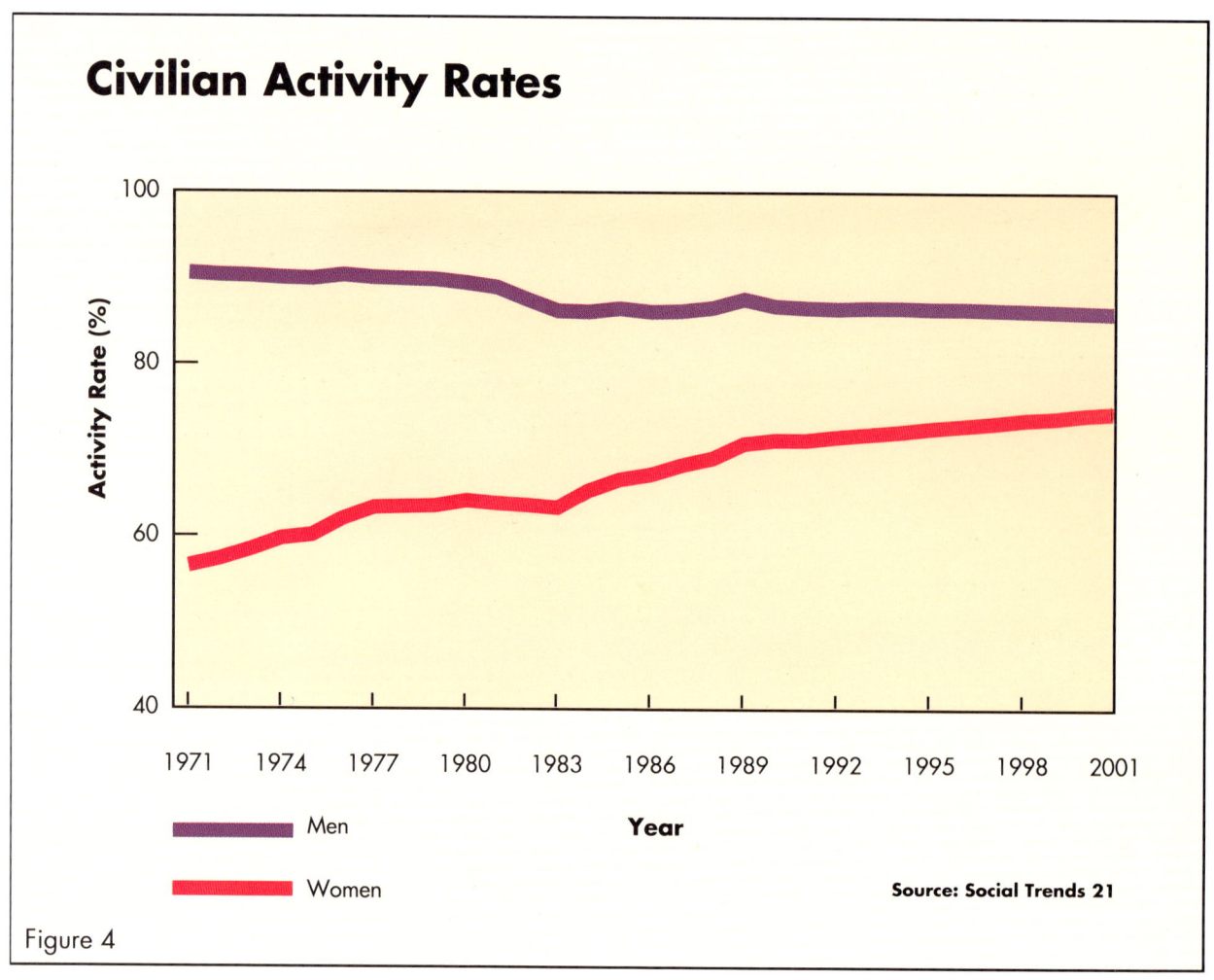

Civilian Activity Rates

Activity Rate (%)

Men

Women

Year

Source: Social Trends 21

Figure 4

Activity Rates

4.14 The effective workforce available to employers is defined as those people either working or actively seeking work. The proportion of people in a given age group who come into this category is known as the activity rate. *Figure 4* above shows the past and projected trends in the overall civilian activity rates for men and women of working age from 1971 to 2001.

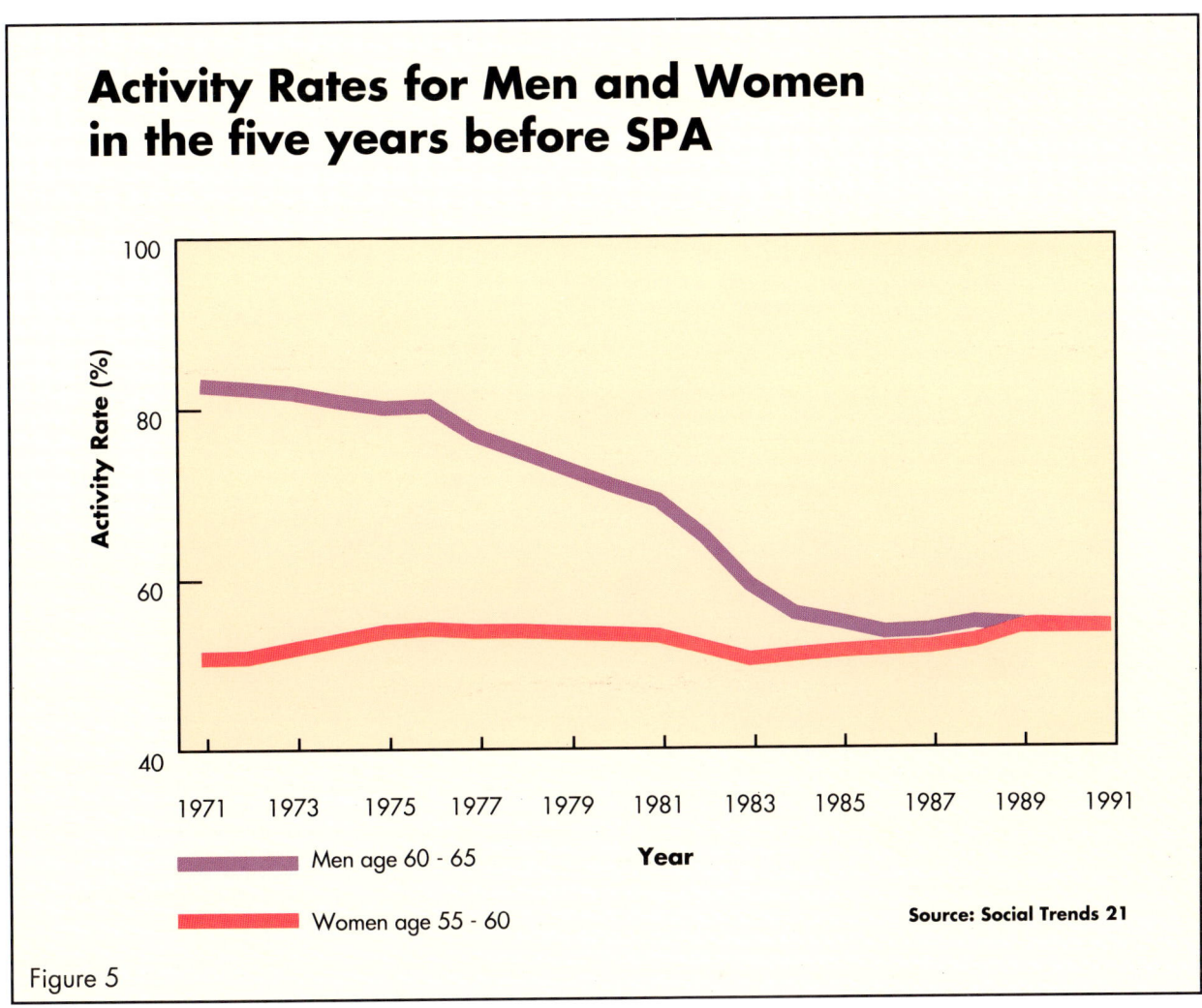

Activity Rates for Men and Women in the five years before SPA

Men age 60 - 65

Women age 55 - 60

Source: Social Trends 21

Figure 5

4.15 For age groups near to state pension age, activity rates are considerably less than 100%. A significant proportion of men and women approaching pension age are receiving benefits such as invalidity benefit or income support. Others have retired before state pension age on occupational pensions. For many years there has been an increasing tendency for men to retire earlier than previously and for women to retire slightly later. *Figure 5* displays this trend and *Figure 6* sets out the position in 1990.

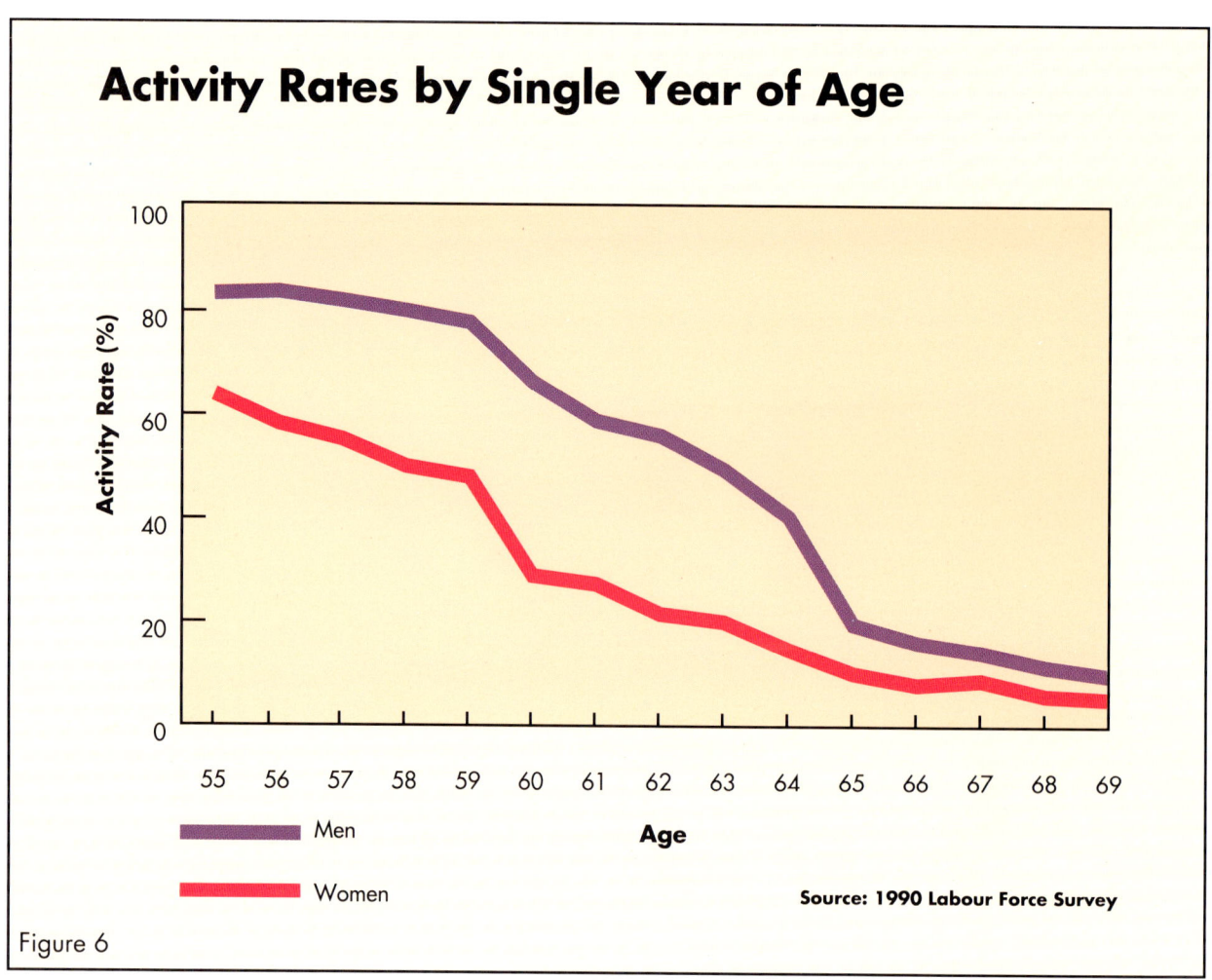

Activity Rates by Single Year of Age

Activity Rate (%) (y-axis: 0, 20, 40, 60, 80, 100)

Age (x-axis: 55, 56, 57, 58, 59, 60, 61, 62, 63, 64, 65, 66, 67, 68, 69)

Men

Women

Source: 1990 Labour Force Survey

Figure 6

Note: **Sample estimates from the LFS estimated by single year of age are subject to greater sampling variability than are estimates for broader age groupings.**

4.16 These changes reflect many different factors including pensioners' increasing income, changes in employment opportunities as employers have tended to shed older workers and part-time working has increased, and changing attitudes to work and leisure. These factors complicate the prediction of activity rates. It has been assumed in the analytical work underpinning this discussion paper that activity rates over the first half of the next century will remain broadly at the levels they are projected to reach in the year 2000.

Life Expectancy

4.17 Life expectancy for those born in 1841 was less than 40 years for a boy but about 43 years for a girl (many children died in infancy). By 1941 life expectancy was 70 years for a boy and about 75 years for a girl (using the Government Actuary's projected mortality rates for years after 1991). Life expectancy for those born 50 years later, in 1991, is about 76 years for a boy and about 81 years for a girl. So people born today can, on average, expect to live about 6 years longer than those born 50 years ago.

4.18 The future expectation of life of those who survive to age 60 or 65 is more relevant to this paper. Over the period 1941 to 1991 life expectancy at age 60 rose by 3.9 years for men and 4.5 years for women. Over the same period, life expectancy at 65 rose by 3.3 years for men and 4.4 years for women. The Government Actuary's projections assume that the increases in longevity in future generations of pensioners will be more modest, but such increases remain part of the reason for the projected growth in pensioner numbers over the next 50 years. The growth is limited because the Government Actuary has assumed that the current high rate of improvement will gradually diminish and that there will be no further reduction in mortality rates after 2029. However, if these projections prove to be too conservative and life expectancy continues to increase, the pensioner population may be higher than presently projected. *(See Appendix 1 paragraphs 42-48.)*

Projected Spending on State Retirement Pension

4.19 This section looks at the projected spending on state retirement pension over the first half of the next century. It also considers how economic growth will affect the economy's ability to support these levels of spending. Each of these aspects is considered briefly below and returned to in *Chapter 6* and *Appendix 1*.

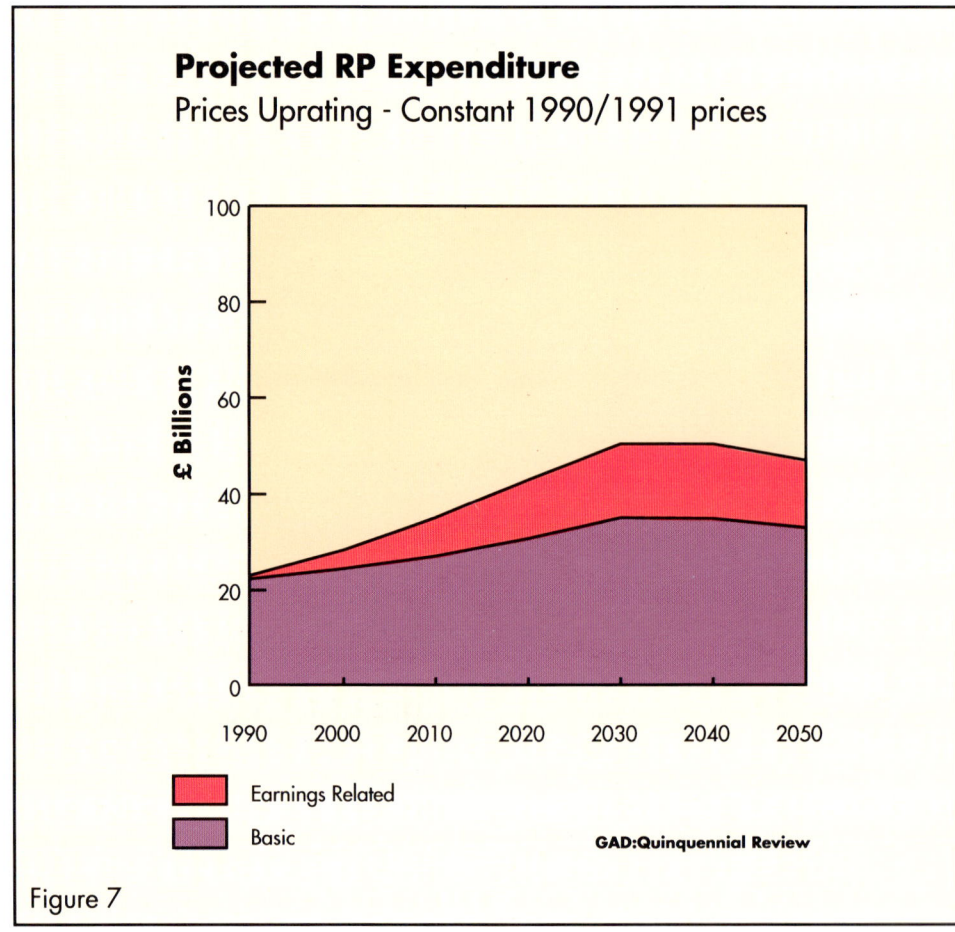

Projected RP Expenditure
Prices Uprating - Constant 1990/1991 prices

Legend:
- Earnings Related
- Basic

GAD:Quinquennial Review

Figure 7

4.20 The main influences on expenditure on state retirement pension over the first half of the next century will be the increasing number of pensioners and the increase in the total amount of SERPS payments. *Figure 7* shows the Government Actuary's projections of the costs of state retirement pension over this period, assuming a 1.5% annual growth of real average earnings. If pensions were to be uprated in line with movements in average earnings, the results would be as set out in *Figure 8*. The figures clearly show the difference in potential cost of prices and earnings uprating of benefits.

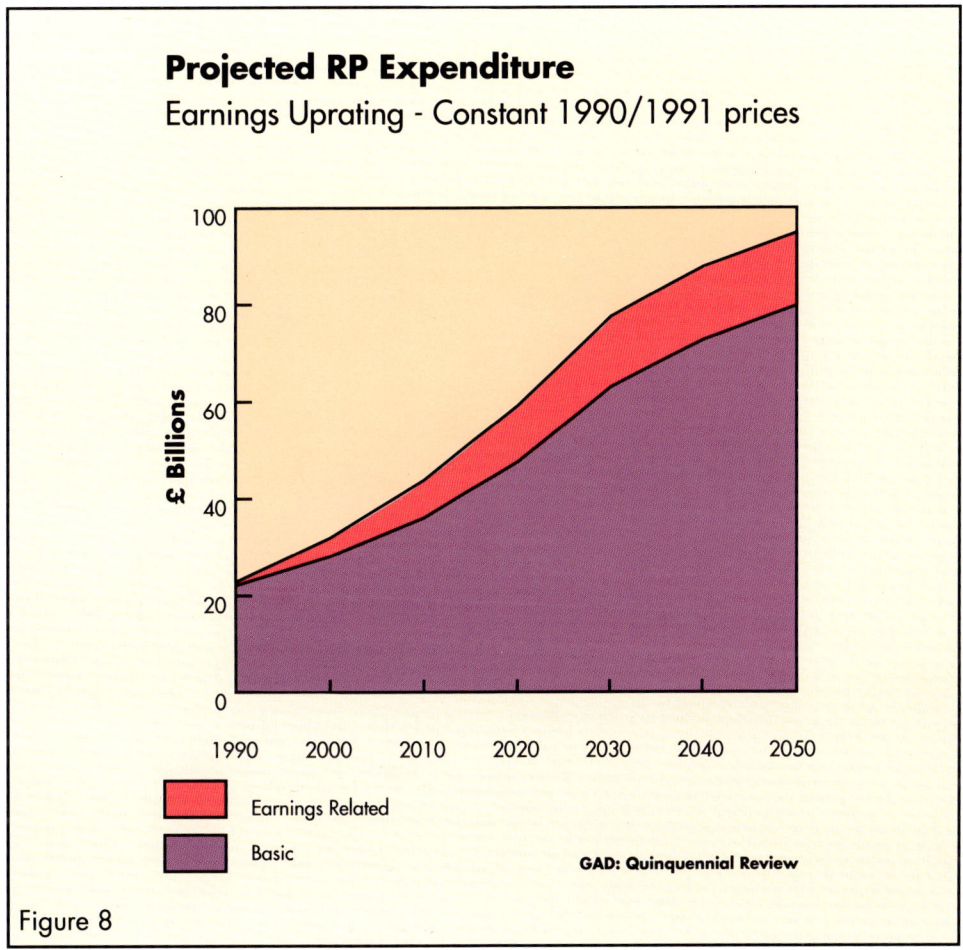

Projected RP Expenditure
Earnings Uprating - Constant 1990/1991 prices

Figure 8

4.21 This rise in spending will not take place against a static level of national income. To view the relative burden imposed by this large rise in the real level of spending in perspective, it is necessary to take economic growth into account. *Figure 9* illustrates this by setting out projected spending on state retirement pensions as a percentage of projected gross domestic product (GDP) for each year shown, on the cautious assumption that GDP grows by 1.5%. *Figure 10* shows how this burden would be affected by moving to a common state pension age of 60, 63 or 65, assuming a prices uprating.

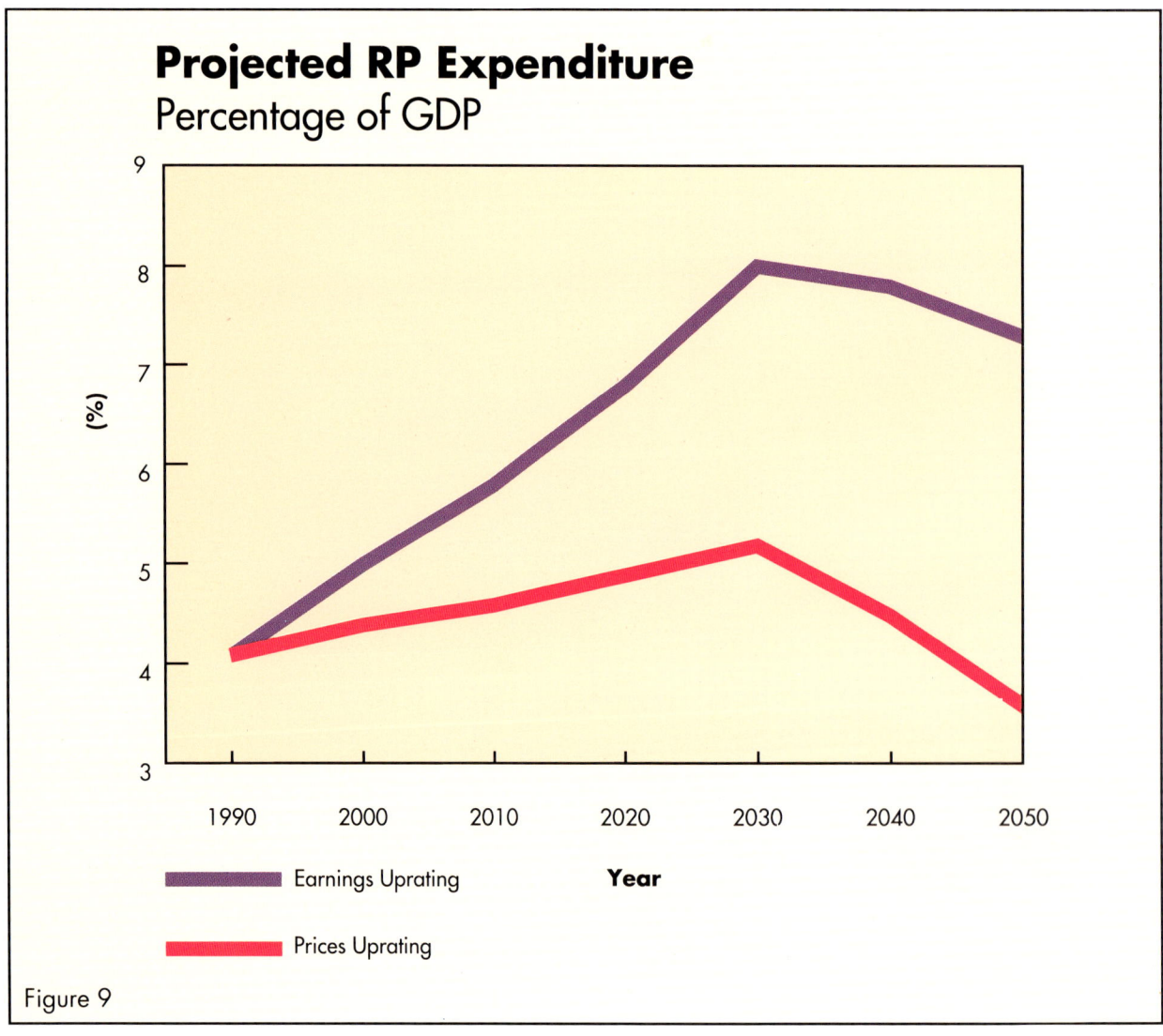

Projected RP Expenditure
Percentage of GDP

Earnings Uprating

Prices Uprating

Year

Figure 9

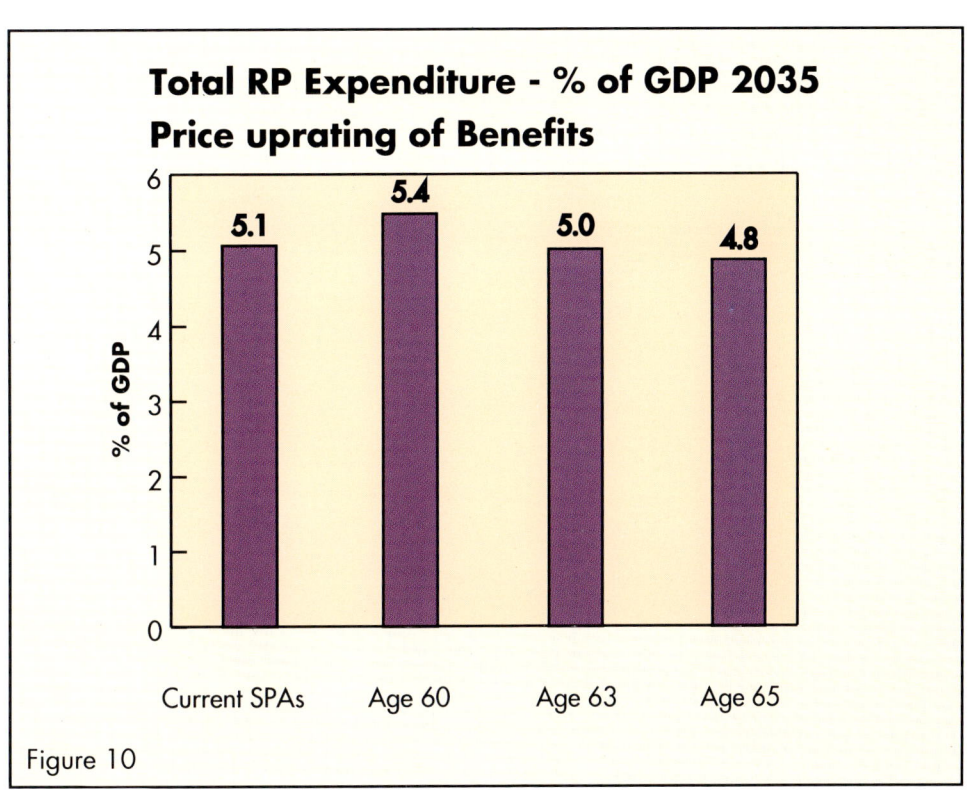

**Total RP Expenditure - % of GDP 2035
Price uprating of Benefits**

Figure 10

5. THE INTERNATIONAL CONTEXT

Introduction

5.1 A number of other countries have already adjusted, or are in the process of adjusting, their state pension schemes in the light of changing circumstances and expectations. This chapter looks at state pension arrangements in those countries that are our main trading partners and competitors.

5.2 The demographic pattern outlined in *Chapter 4* is found in most other countries of the developed world. The combined effects of low fertility rates and increasing life expectancy are serving to slow the rate of population growth and increase considerably the proportion of elderly people in the population.

5.3 There are, however, differences in the size and timing of the increase in the proportion of elderly people. In the UK the proportion of people over 65 is expected to rise from 14.9% in 1980 to 20.4% by 2040, whilst in France it starts from a slightly lower base (14%) but is expected to rise to 22.7% by 2040. The proportion of people aged 65 or more in Japan will more than double in the next 40 years.

Changes Made Abroad

European Community

5.4 The European Council have in the past approved two Directives which deal with the implementation of equal treatment in pension schemes. These are Directives 79/7/EEC which covered state schemes and 86/378/EEC which covered occupational schemes. Both of these Directives specifically allowed for the continuation of unequal pension ages. However, the European Court's ruling in the Barber judgement (Barber v Guardian Royal Exchange C 262/88) has overturned elements of Directive 86/378. The current situation requires clarification from cases currently before the European Court of Justice. The European Commission has also proposed a new Directive with the aim of completing the implementation of equal treatment in state and occupational pension schemes. The new Directive would cover the areas specifically excluded from earlier legislation, such as pension age, survivors' benefits, dependency benefits, individual benefits and family benefits. The draft was originally introduced in 1987. A number of Member States, including the UK, had concerns about the draft, and an amended version was considered in 1989. Concerns remained and no further action was taken until June 1991, when the Commission re-opened consultations with Member States, which are continuing.

5.5 Many of our EC partners have already moved to equal pension ages for men and women or are moving towards equalisation. Over the next two decades most will have introduced equal state pension ages, many at age

65 or above. The following paragraphs examine the position in Italy, Germany and France.

5.6   Italy spends a very high proportion of GDP - 11.1% in 1987 - on pensions. The working population is projected to fall by 15% by the year 2040, whilst the number of elderly people is set to increase by 35% over the same period. Partly as a result of these factors the Italian Government is in the process of developing proposals which would raise pension age to 65 for both sexes, increase contributions and lengthen the period of working life used to calculate pension entitlement. Current plans include a series of one-year increments in pension age every three years starting in 1993. This would fully equalise pension age at 65 by 2016.

5.7   Germany has also adopted measures to move towards an equal pension age. A pension reform was announced in 1988 and will be implemented from 1992. Minimum pension age will be increased by 3 months a year from 2001 to 2004 and by 6 months a year from 2005 to 2012. This will result in a common pension age of 65 by 2012. Other measures include indexing pensions to net (rather than gross) salary increases, increasing the contribution from general taxation, and widening the coverage of income liable to contributions.

5.8   This reform was prompted, in part, by the demographic figures and trends of a pre-reunification Germany. Now that the younger population of the former Democratic Republic has been absorbed the position may be different, although the birth rates of the two former Germanys are beginning to converge. However, there are, at present, no proposals to modify the pension reform programme.

5.9   France introduced pension reforms in the early 1980s which effectively reduced the minimum age for full pension to age 60. Over the period 1980-2040 the proportion of people over age 65 is set to rise from 14% to 22.7%, coupled with a projected decrease in the size of the working population. These demographic projections have prompted the Government to reopen the question of pension reform with the recent publication of a White Paper on the way forward for state pension provision. However, as yet there are no proposals to change pension age.

5.10   Support ratios (here defined as the ratio of the population aged 15-64 to the number of people aged 65 or over) are projected to decline throughout the EC. The most severe change takes place in the Netherlands where the ratio falls from 5.7 in 1980 to 2.3 in 2040. This compares with a change from 4.3 to 3.0 over the same period in the UK using the same measure. Comparisons of the support ratios in 2040 for Member States of the European Community and also the USA, Japan and New Zealand are shown in the tables at the end of this chapter. *(NOTE: These ratios are on a different basis from those shown in Chapter 4 in order to provide direct comparison with other Member States. The earlier figures are for Great*

Britain and show the ratio of the working population to pensioners (i.e. women over 60 and men over 65). However, information was not available to provide support ratios on this basis for other Member States.)

Other European Countries

5.11   The position on pension age is not quite the same in the rest of Europe. In Norway pension age is 67 for both sexes. Changes to pension provision are being considered. In a recent review of the social security system the Government reaffirmed its commitment to 67. The other Scandinavian countries and Cyprus have equal state pension ages at 65, whilst other countries still have unequal pension ages. This varies from 60 for men and 53 to 57 for women in Czechoslovakia; 60 for men and 55 for women in Hungary, Yugoslavia, Bulgaria, and Romania; 61 for men and 60 for women in Malta; 65 for men and 60 for women in Poland and Austria; to 65 for men and 62 for women in Switzerland.

Non-European Countries

The United States of America

5.12   The proportion of people over 65 in the United States is expected to grow from 11.3% in 1980 to a peak of 19.8% in 2040. Social security reforms were introduced in 1983 to restore the short-term and long-term viability of the pensions system. The reform package included a number of changes which are to be implemented between 1983 and 2027.

5.13   An increase in pension age will be phased in in two stages. Over the period 2003 to 2009 pension age will increase to 66 and then, from 2021 to 2027, to 67. The earliest age at which retirement benefits can be drawn will remain at 62 but the reduction in pensions taken at that age will be increased from 20% to 30%.

5.14   Measures have also been introduced to increase revenue by raising contribution rates, the increments for deferred retirement have been increased to encourage older workers to remain in employment, and the tariff rules on earned income for beneficiaries between ages 65-69 have been relaxed.

Japan

5.15   The demographic pressures facing Japan are more severe than those of the UK. Whilst the population is still relatively young, it is ageing much faster because life expectancy is so high and the fertility rate quite low. The proportion of people over 65 is set to rise from 9.1% in 1980 to 22.7% in 2040. Because of this and the relative immaturity of pension schemes in Japan, reforms to public pension provision were introduced in 1986.

5.16 The reforms have three main features: unification of the three main pension schemes to reduce the differences between them leading to a common benefit and contribution structure; providing a universal flat-rate basic amount to all elderly people in the country through the National Pension Scheme; and adjustments to the benefit level. Pension age will be equalised by raising pension age for women from 56 to 60 by the year 2000. A subsequent increase for both sexes to age 65 is planned.

Table 1: State Pension Ages - International Comparisons i) European Community						
Country	Current Standard Pension Age		Planned Standard Pension Age		Effective Date	Support Ratio in 1980*	Support Ratio in 2040*
	M	F	M	F			
Belgium	Flexible Pension Age 60-65		–	–		4.5	2.7
Denmark	67	67	–	–		4.4	2.3
France	60	60	–	–		4.5	2.6
Germany[1]	63	60	65	65	Phased in by 2012	4.2	2.0
Greece	65	60	–	–		4.8	2.9
Republic of Ireland	66	66	–	–		5.4	3.6
Italy	60	55	65	65	Plans to equalise by 2016	4.7	2.4
Luxembourg	65	65	–	–		5.0	2.8
Netherlands	65	65	–	–		5.7	2.3
Portugal	65	62	–	–		6.1	3.0
Spain	65	65	–	–		5.8	2.6
UK	65	60	–	–		4.3	3.0

[1] State pension age is 65 but because of early retirement provisions the effective ages are 63 for men and 60 for women. Pension ages will be raised gradually from 2001 until fully equalised at 65 by 2012.

Table 2: State Pension Ages - International Comparisons ii) Other Countries							
Country	Current Standard Pension Age		Planned Standard Pension Age		Effective Date	Support Ratio in 1980*	Support Ratio in 2040*
	M	F	M	F			
USA	65	65	67	67	Phased in by 2027	5.8	3.0
Japan	60	56	60	60	Phased in by 2000 then possibly increased to 65	7.4	2.6
New Zealand	60	60	65	65	Phased in by 2001	6.4	2.7

*   The support ratios in these two tables are on the basis described in *paragraph 5.10.*

Acknowledgement:

The information contained in this chapter has been drawn in part from the following publications:

•   'Reforming Public Pensions', published by OECD, Paris, 1988;

•   'Ageing Populations: The Social Policy Implications', published by OECD, Paris 1988.

We are grateful to the OECD for agreeing to the publication of this material.

6. A COMMON STATE PENSION AGE

Introduction

6.1   The choice of a fixed common pension age would affect future state pension entitlements; would either incur costs or secure savings for the National Insurance Fund and the Exchequer and for individual contributors; and would have wider economic consequences. Many of our competitor countries either have already, or are proposing, a common pension age. These range from 60, the current level in France, to 67, the current level in Denmark. As is indicated in the preceding chapter, a number of countries are reviewing levels of state pension age, not only on grounds of equality but because of the long term economic cost of seeking to sustain current patterns of provision. No major country is proposing a reduction in fixed levels of pension age. A number of our principal competitors are implementing increases. For example, Germany plans equalisation at 65; the United States at 67. Japan is now phasing in an increase to a common level of 60, but a subsequent move for both sexes to age 65 is proposed. The decision taken in every country will have an impact on its economic competitiveness in the 21st Century. No country can determine its policy in isolation from what may be under consideration by its competitors.

6.2   Circumstances in the United Kingdom are, however, not identical to those elsewhere. The ratio of those in work to those over retirement age will be less favourable in the UK in coming decades than in other countries. There is no reason why the UK should inevitably have to conform to the general international trend, or to settle at any specific point in the current span of common state pension ages. Nevertheless, we do face the prospect of an increasing dependent population. The financial and economic effects of various options are described in this chapter. Three of the possible options in the present international range are illustrated; 60 (the current pension age for women); 63; and 65 (the current pension age for men).

Effects On Pension Entitlement

Claiming a Pension

6.3   Moving to a common state pension age would change the minimum age at which either men or women or both could claim their state retirement pension. This would apply both to the basic pension and to any SERPS. Assuming that the maximum age for national insurance contributions for employees remained linked to pension age, there would be corresponding changes in their contribution liabilities.

6.4   If, as now, anyone working beyond state pension age could still claim their state pension, or alternatively increase its value by earning increments *(see paragraph 2.20)*, the effects of reducing men's pension age would be broadly as follows:

- A common pension age below 65 would mean that men could claim their pension earlier than at present and, whether working or not, would not have to pay national insurance contributions after the new pension age.

- About 14% of men currently continue in paid work for at least a year after age 65. The proportion who would continue working beyond a pension age below 65 might well be higher.

- Men who would have retired before age 65 whether or not their pension age had changed would be able to top up any other retirement income with their state pension. At present about 46% of men aged 60 to 64 have left the workforce and are effectively retired.

- A pension age below 65 would open up the option of earlier retirement for those men who would have retired at 65 but could now afford to retire sooner.

6.5 A common pension age above 60 would mean that women could not claim their pension until later than at present and, if working, would have to pay national insurance contributions. Of women in their sixtieth year about half are in paid work and of these about 40% retire shortly afterwards. A higher state pension age would presumably reduce that proportion.

Entitlement to Basic Pension

6.6 A person's entitlement to basic pension depends on the number of *"qualifying years"* they have earned over their working life by paying, or being credited with, national insurance contributions. The number of qualifying years they need is related to pension age, and is therefore different for men and women. To be entitled to a basic pension at the full rate, a woman needs 39 qualifying years and a man 44. Assuming that the underlying rules of entitlement were not changed, a common pension age of 60 would reduce the number of qualifying years for a man to 39; a common pension age of 65 would increase a woman's qualifying years to 44; and a common pension age of 63 would mean 42 qualifying years for both sexes.

Entitlement to SERPS

6.7 SERPS is based on an individual's earnings since 1978, revalued to reflect the movement in national average earnings in the period up to state pension age. Women who continued in paid employment after age 60 as a result of an increase in their state pension age would be entitled to a different level of SERPS if their earnings in the years past 60 differed significantly from their previous earnings. Any increase in entitlement (which is likely to be unusual) would rarely, if ever, compensate for the combined effect of having to claim their pension later and pay additional years of national insurance contributions. By the same rule, virtually all men who ceased work sooner, as a result of the decrease in their pension age, would find that earlier entitlement would more than outweigh any resulting difference in the level of SERPS payable.

Costs or Savings to the Exchequer

6.8   *Appendix 1* sets out in detail a range of estimates of the costs or savings which would arise from adopting different state pension ages, expressed in terms of their impact on the Exchequer. For illustrative purposes, the estimates relate to possible common pension ages of 60, 63 or 65, and assume that the present structure of benefits and contributions remains unchanged. *Appendix 3* sets out the other assumptions on which the estimates are based.

6.9   Much depends on the date at which the costs and savings are assessed. The number of people aged 60 to 64, the group affected by the changes, peaks at around 2025, falling away again after that. SERPS expenditure peaks at about the same time. The year 2025 is therefore a useful indicator of the peak level of the financial effects of changing state pension ages. The year 2035 has been adopted to illustrate the scale of these effects over the longer term.

6.10   On the central assumptions set out in *Appendix 1,* the annual Exchequer costs and savings over the first half of the next century are estimated at 1991 prices to be:

Table 4: Equalised state pension age costs or savings (£ Billions)			
	60	**63**	**65**
2025	$4\frac{1}{2}$	-1.0	$-3\frac{1}{2}$
2035	$3\frac{1}{2}$	$-\frac{1}{2}$	-3.0

There is a great deal of uncertainty about these estimated figures, as is explained in *Appendix 1, paragraphs 42-48.* But they do illustrate the order of magnitude involved. These costs and savings are smaller than the corresponding increases and reductions in pensions expenditure because there would be offsetting savings and costs in expenditure on other social security benefits and income tax revenue.

6.11   These estimates assume that the state pension, together with the upper and lower earnings limits for national insurance contributions, are uprated annually in line with movements in prices. To illustrate the possible range of

6.30 The structure of the phasing would also need to be settled. One approach would be to phase the change in by years - one year in two, one in three, or whatever rate was chosen. For illustrative purposes, *Table 5* shows what would happen to women's pension ages if they were moved from 60 to 65 at the rate of one year in two, beginning with people born in 1950. On this basis the change to age 65 would take nine years, as those born in 1954 reached the new pension age in 2019. Phasing at the rate of one year in three would take 13 years, one in four would take 17 years, and so on.

Table 5						
Pension Age						
Year of Birth	**60**	**61**	**62**	**63**	**64**	**65**
1949	**2009**					
1950		**2011**				
1951			**2013**			
1952				**2015**		
1953					**2017**	
1954						**2019**
1955						**2020**

6.31 Phasing by years would be the simplest approach both to understand and to administer. On the other hand, it would create some sharp differences between people who were close together in age. Phasing as in *Table 5*, for example, would mean that a woman born in December 1950 would be entitled to her state pension in December 2011, but a woman born in January 1951 would not be entitled to her pension until January 2013. These differences would become correspondingly sharper if the phasing were extended to one year in three or one in four.

6.32 A smoother approach would be to phase the change in by months. Taking the year 2010 as an illustrative starting date, a rate of one month in two would mean, for example, that:

- a woman born in January 1950 would get her pension in February 2010;

- a woman born in February 1950 would get her pension in April 2010;

- a woman born in March 1950 would get her pension in June 2010;

and so on. On this basis the phasing-in period would last ten years at one month in two, 15 years at one month in three, and so on.

6.33 The same options apply in principle to phasing in any other common pension age, but the time needed to reach age 63 - or any other age from 61 to 64 - would be correspondingly shorter. For age 60, employers would need to be given a period - such as five years - in which to prepare for the new arrangements, after which the new common state pension age could in principle be introduced immediately.

Costs

6.34 The Exchequer costs of equalising state pension age quoted in *paragraph 6.10* assume that the new age is phased in beginning in 2010. These costs would vary if a different timetable were chosen. The costs in the short to medium term during and immediately following any phasing period clearly depend critically upon the year in which the new age is phased in and the timetable for phasing, as well as on the number of people at the ages affected in the relevant years.

6.35 The precise costs vary from option to option and depend on resolving a number of questions, including the timing of the alignment of contracting-out terms with the new pension ages and the treatment of previously accrued Guaranteed Minimum Pensions and their interaction with SERPS. Resolving these complex questions could involve significant additional Exchequer costs in the short to medium term. Adjustments of contributions to contracted-out occupational pension schemes will also be a significant factor which would tend to amplify the macro-economic effect. In the longer term these extra costs would fall away.

6.36 If people have enough notice of the new pension age they will be able to adjust their plans, including their commitments and savings, accordingly. Employers and occupational schemes will be able to adapt their arrangements as well which should ease the labour market transition to the new pension ages. If they have only a short amount of notice, the behavioural effects could be different and this would also affect the short term costs.

7. A FLEXIBLE STATE PENSION AGE

Introduction

7.1 It would be possible to adopt a state pension scheme which offered benefits to men and women on an equal basis but had no fixed pension age. A scheme of this kind might be seen as having one or both of two objectives: to make it easier for people to retire earlier if they so wished, by lowering or removing the minimum age at which a state pension became payable; or to make it more advantageous for people to continue working longer, by offering better pensions when they did retire.

7.2 Some possible schemes are discussed below - a variable rate scheme; a split scheme with SERPS and basic pension paid at different ages; and a contribution test scheme. Other schemes have been suggested elsewhere. Some occupational pension schemes, for example, allow people to select the level of their pension provision and pay correspondingly more or less in contributions. It might be possible to operate a similar nominated option scheme in the state sector. The National Association of Pension Funds has also proposed a flexible state scheme for those in receipt of an occupational pension.

7.3 All flexible schemes require detailed and complex administrative frameworks, which can be constructed only once the precise details are established. This paper does not explore this aspect but concentrates on the broad issues involved. For the same reason, financial costings have not been produced though it seems likely that any scheme offering lower rates of pension could lead to higher expenditure on income-related benefits.

Flexibilities in the Existing State Scheme

7.4 Some people already retire before state pension age. Many others defer their retirement and continue to work beyond state pension age. *(See paragraphs 2.16-2.20.)*

7.5 Retirement before pension age is clearly easier for people who have other sources of income. *Figure 1* in *Chapter 3* shows how pensioners' incomes grew between 1979 and 1988, highlighting the importance of the growth in income from occupational pensions and savings.

7.6 Occupational pension schemes may themselves be more flexible than the state pension scheme, at least in terms of when the pension can be drawn. A 1990 survey by the National Association of Pension Funds showed that a majority of occupational schemes covered by the survey had early retirement provisions, and a quarter of these offered benefits on early retirement more favourable than normal actuarial reductions would imply. Nearly all occupational pension schemes must now allow members to improve the level of benefits available to them by making additional voluntary contributions which, in some cases, may also facilitate early retirement.

7.7 Personal pensions contribute further to flexibility, and personal pensions in excess of the protected rights element can commence from age 50. Some flexibility is also available to men with little or no potential income other than the state retirement pension. *(See paragraphs 2.16 - 2.18.)*

Scope For Additional Flexibility

7.8 Additional flexibility for women, given their current state pension age, could be achieved only at considerable extra cost. The main scope for additional flexibility in the state pension scheme lies in facilitating earlier retirement among men. The scope is, in practice, quite limited for three groups of men; first, those who would be dependent on income support whenever they retired (although more might be encouraged to claim retirement pension and income support earlier under a flexible scheme); second, those who would be entitled to an invalidity pension; and third, those whose income from other sources is such that the level of state retirement pension is not a decisive factor in their decision to retire.

7.9 The main beneficiaries of greater flexibility would be men whose potential income as pensioners is above income support levels but low enough for access to a state pension to make the difference between working and retiring. As the total amount of SERPS in payment to all pensioners increases, this group should grow in size relative to those receiving income support.

A Variable Rate Scheme

7.10 The type of variable rate scheme most commonly canvassed is a *"decade of retirement"* between the ages of 60 and 70[1]. The basic principle of this type of scheme is to offer people a trade-off between the size of their pension and the age from which they claim it. Those retiring at age 60 would be entitled to the lowest rate of pension, as it would on average remain in payment over the longest period; those retiring at 70 would be entitled to the highest rate of pension; and graded rates of pension would be available at each age in between. The same principle could obviously be applied to any other period (e.g. ages 63-73) with consequent effects on the cost of the scheme.

7.11 The fairest trade-off between age and pension entitlement would be achieved by calculating the increments between ages on an actuarially neutral basis. Assuming basic pension is uprated in line with prices this would give gradually increasing rates of increment, ranging from about 7.3% between ages 60 and 61 to about 9.8% between 69 and 70.

---

[1]This was recently recommended in 1989 by the House of Lords Select Committee on the European Communities, in their report 'Equal Treatment for Men and Women in Pensions and Other Benefits' (HL Paper 51).

7.12 To illustrate the effects of this approach on basic pension entitlement, *Table 6* shows what levels of pension could be claimed at each age, rounded to the nearest pound, if the present full rate of £52 were to be reached either at age 63 or at age 65 - sometimes referred to as the *'pivotal'* age. Entitlement to SERPS could be calculated in a similar way, with the full rate available from the *'pivotal'* age.

Table 6: Basic pension available at different ages (£) (Source: GAD, assumes prices uprating and single person's pension rates)											
Age											
	60	61	62	63	64	65	66	67	68	69	70
Age 63 'Pivot'	£42	£45	£48	£52	£56	£61	£66	£72	£78	£86	£94
Age 65 'Pivot'	£36	£38	£41	£45	£48	£52	£56	£61	£67	£73	£81

7.13 The costs of these two options vary considerably.

Long-term Costs or Savings

7.14 The long-term costs incurred or savings generated by such a scheme would depend primarily on the overall levels of pension available. In this section 'long term' refers to the period at least 20 years after implementation.

- **Retirement Pension Expenditure**
  Because the increments are actuarially neutral, the two examples in *Table 6* would generate long-term savings in retirement pension expenditure at least comparable to those generated, respectively, by common pension ages of 63 and 65 *(see paragraph 6.10)*.

- **Income Related Benefit Expenditure**
  On the other hand, any variable rate scheme would tend to incur additional short and long-term costs to the extent that people claimed their pension below the *'pivotal'* age and found themselves, then or later, eligible for income support or other income-related benefits. These costs might be somewhat reduced over time as the total amount of SERPS in payment to all pensioners increased, and would also be lower in so far as people took themselves above income support levels by claiming a larger pension later or as a result of receiving an occupational pension.

7.15 A variable rate scheme with a minimum age of 60 would offer real, additional flexibility to men who could retire earlier if they were able to augment other sources of income with a reduced state pension. After implementation it would offer men and women a fair trade-off between the size of pension and the age at which it is first drawn.

7.16 By comparison with a pension age above 60, it would offer women too the possibility of claiming an earlier pension. However, this would mean the pension being paid at a permanently reduced rate. In addition, the scheme would have substantial start-up costs as men took up the option of earlier pensions. These would start at about £2-3 billion a year, falling gradually thereafter.

7.17 Much of this money would go to people who would have retired anyway or had done so already. Such evidence as exists suggests that people would be more likely to claim their pension sooner than to claim it later, with potentially adverse effects on the size of the labour force as well as on income-related benefit costs. If they could still claim their pension and remain in work, many men would be able to top up their earned income with an earlier state pension. So the scheme would tend generally to offer either greater flexibility or higher incomes to relatively well-off men, whilst encouraging the less well-off - men and women - to work longer. The labour market effects would be less pronounced than, but possibly quite close to, those for equalisation at 60. It is difficult to assess the costs of such a scheme. The retirement pension costs would be lower than those of a fixed age of 60 in the short term, but there would also probably be many more people, particularly women, in receipt of income-related benefits.

Possible Adjustments

7.18 A variable rate scheme could be adjusted to alter some of the problems of the basic model. Increments could be set at a level below the actuarially neutral rate, so that the levels of pension available were higher at the younger ages and lower at the older ages. For any given 'pivotal' age this would increase the scope for those less well-off to retire earlier whilst also reducing the numbers who would become dependent on income-related benefits. But this approach would mean that the lower level of increments would result in a weaker incentive to delay retirement, with an adverse impact on the size of the labour force; would increase the retirement pension costs (or decrease the savings) for any given 'pivotal' age; and would offer an unfair return for delaying a claim to pension beyond age 60.

7.19   Increments could be set at a level above the actuarially neutral rate. This would reduce the start-up costs and strengthen the incentive to work longer. But this incentive would still bite hardest on the least well-off. Also, for any given *'pivotal'* age, bigger increments would produce lower pensions at younger ages and would therefore be less effective in facilitating earlier retirement.

7.20   Those whose pension came into payment before the *'pivotal'* age could become entitled at a later age - say 75 - to the rate of basic pension available at the *'pivotal'* age. This would obviously add to the costs (or reduce the savings), although it would be less expensive than a common pension age of 60. The effect would be to bring most people up to the rate of basic pension at age 75 that they would have received under the present scheme whilst still offering additional flexibility to men in their early 60s.

A Split Retirement Pension Scheme

7.21   A split retirement pension scheme would introduce some of the features of a variable rate scheme whilst retaining a fixed pension age. SERPS would become payable at age 60 and the basic pension at age 65. It would then be the earlier availability of SERPS, rather than the availability of reduced rates of both basic pension and SERPS, which facilitated earlier retirement for men. Because the bulk of pensions expenditure is on basic pension, this approach would be at least broadly cost-neutral in the longer term, but there would be short-term costs.

7.22   A scheme of this kind would have two advantages by comparison with a variable rate scheme. First, many contracted-out occupational schemes offer pensions at 60. A pension age of 60 for SERPS would enable others also to claim an earnings-related pension then or, alternatively, to defer it in favour of earning increments from a higher age. Secondly, it would mean that the full rate of basic pension would be available to everyone from age 65, thereby avoiding the permanently reduced pensions which would result from early claims under a variable rate scheme.

7.23   On the other hand, by offering no basic pension at all below age 65, a split retirement pension scheme would offer less flexibility to those on relatively low earnings, and would tend if anything to skew the benefits of greater flexibility still further towards men rather than women. It could also create difficulties for occupational schemes with equal pension ages above age 60, as they would face pressure to make pensions payable from the earlier age.

A Contribution Test Scheme

7.24   A contribution test would be a quite distinct alternative to a variable rate scheme. It would base entitlement to basic pension and SERPS solely on a contribution test. This paper focuses on how the basic pension might work.

7.25   Projecting people's future contribution records is an enormously complex task and no detailed analysis of the effects of different types of scheme and their financial consequences can be attempted without it. This section of the paper therefore only briefly outlines one possible approach.

7.26   At present both men and women can reach the number of 'qualifying years' required for a full basic pension - 44 and 39 respectively - up to five years before the minimum age at which they can draw it. The simplest form of contribution test scheme would specify a common number of qualifying years for both men and women with no minimum age for payment of pension.

7.27   People would have to be able to retire and draw a basic pension on less than the number of qualifying years needed for full entitlement. If this were not possible those who happened to have a significantly deficient contribution record would be forced either to continue working long after everyone else or to retire without any basic pension at all. To have a neutral effect on the costs of the scheme, the pension might need to be reduced actuarially for each year by which a person's contribution record fell short of the number of qualifying years specified for entitlement to a full pension. A reduced pension could then be claimed at any age at which the relevant number of qualifying years had been reached.

7.28   Provision for increments could be retained for people who wished to continue working, and to defer drawing their pension, after they had attained the number of qualifying years needed for a full pension. If the rate of increments were set so as to keep them actuarially neutral, there would be no particular reason to limit the number of years over which increments could be earned.

Some Implications of a Contribution Test Scheme

7.29   It would be possible to introduce a minimum age - say 60 - below which the basic pension could not be claimed, although only at the expense of flexibility below the chosen age.

7.30   If a contribution test scheme were to be significantly less expensive than a common pension age of 60, the number of qualifying years needed for a full pension is likely to be more than the 44 years currently required by men.

7.31 People who might receive much lower pensions, in comparison with straightforward equalisation, would be those who reached their 60s with a significant deficiency in their contribution record:

- people who had spent periods out of paid work or with earnings below the lower earnings limit for national insurance contribution purposes. The effects on people in the former category might be ameliorated as Home Responsibilities Protection matures over time.;

- people coming or returning from countries without adequate reciprocal pension arrangements; and

- others with gaps in their contribution records which they have not made good by means of voluntary contributions.

Flexible Schemes: Common Features

7.32 Each of the three schemes described in this chapter share some common features:

- in general, men would be best placed to take most advantage of the flexibility on offer;

- any scheme which makes it possible for individuals to retire earlier on reduced pensions would lead to more pensioners becoming dependent on income-related benefits;

- any scheme with a minimum age below 63 is likely to incur short term costs;

- any scheme which gives greater flexibility by allowing people to retire at an earlier age than at present would tend to incur economic consequences of the kind, if not on the scale, associated with equalisation at that earlier age; and

- such schemes are complex to administer for employers, individuals and government. They could increase the difficulties for employers in deciding their retirement policies. Individuals would have to make complex choices, which could prove not to be in their best interests in the long term. Such schemes would be more complex to administer than those with a set, common pension age.

7.33 Each of the schemes meets, to some extent, the objectives set out at the beginning of this chapter:

- a variable rate scheme would enable individuals to retire earlier if they wished by lowering the minimum age at which state pension became payable and compensate them for working longer by offering better pensions. But the reduction in pensions drawn earlier than the pivotal age would be quite substantial in cash terms and the benefits of this type of scheme would fall mainly to relatively well off men. There would also be substantial start-up costs; and possibly long term costs if some of those drawing reduced pensions relied on income-related benefits to make up the difference;

- in comparison, under a contribution test scheme, people with a significantly deficient contribution record - who would be mainly women - might receive substantially lower pensions than under a common pension age;

- a split retirement pension scheme would offer less flexibility than the other two, but would largely remove the problem of leaving more people dependent on income-related benefits for long periods which would be a feature of the other two schemes.

8. CONCLUSION: THE ISSUES FOR DEBATE

8.1 As in our competitor countries, Britain's population is ageing. People are living longer thanks to better diet, healthier working conditions and improved medical techniques, including preventative measures. This trend is set to continue into the next century, when there will be also be fewer people of working age, because fewer children are being born. It is a trend which will pose a growing challenge for the economic management of all industrialised countries over coming decades.

8.2 As illustrated in *Chapter 5*, many of our international competitors are adjusting their retirement plans to provide for state pensions to become available at later ages, up to and, in some cases beyond the age of 65, so that they will have bigger workforces to supply pension benefits for their retirement populations. None of our major competitors is making, or proposing, any reduction in its current state pension age for either men or women.

8.3 Elderly people rightly expect to be able to maintain a reasonable standard of living in their retirement. SERPS ensures that an increasing number of people receive higher pensions when they retire. Resources for these better pensions will have to be provided by a proportionately smaller number of working people, whether they are paid as state pensions or from private savings during retired people's working lives. There is therefore a case for following the international trend towards encouraging later retirement.

8.4 On the other hand, the UK may be less seriously affected by these developments than some other countries. Our demographic pattern seems likely to be less dramatically shifted than, for example, in Japan or Germany. And we have already made encouraging progress towards occupational and private provision of pension benefits for the elderly, so that the drain on the Exchequer may be less severe.

8.5 The evidence is that, when they have the choice, people like to retire as soon as they can. This trend has been particularly marked among men over 60 over the last couple of decades, when many of them have stopped work in their early 60s without waiting for the state pension age of 65. The reasons for this pattern have been complex, including structural adjustments in the labour market, the growth of alternative sources of income in retirement in addition to the state pension, more resources for leisure pursuits, and greater awareness of the dangers of impaired health. It is not clear how far such forces will continue to bear on retirement decisions in the future, although it is anticipated that the growth in additional retirement income from occupational and personal provision will, on present policies, continue.

8.6 It will be necessary to strike a judgement on the right course to take in equalising the state pension age, taking account of these somewhat conflicting considerations. At this stage the Government has reached no conclusions.

8.7 The financial and economic effects of different options will also be important. Choosing a relatively low common pension age, say at 60, would have an adverse effect on the economy and the Exchequer. A higher age, probably any age above 63, could lead to higher national output and would offer opportunities for lowering taxation or improving public services, for example, by raising the level of the state pension. The costs of equalising at 60 are largely the result of paying pensions to men earlier, and the savings from equalising at 65 are largely the result of paying pensions to women later.

8.8 There would be some attractions in allowing working people some flexibility in their choice of state pension age, following what has in practice been happening in many occupational schemes and in some of our competitor countries. But flexible state pension provision could also mean greater complexity and costs, for employers and occupational pension schemes as well as the Exchequer. It could also leave a greater number of pensioners, particularly women, dependent on state income-related benefits in their old age.

8.9 Whatever solutions are adopted, the Government is clear that it would not be right to continue with unequal pension ages for men and women. There have been immense social and economic changes since these ages were set at their present levels over half a century ago. These changes include the greater willingness of women of all ages and marital status to work, and the spread of part time working. At the same time pensioners generally have been living longer, and have gradually become better off through the development of occupational pensions. To have differing pension ages as now is increasingly out of line with developments in the equal treatment of men and women in the employment field, including in occupational pension schemes.

8.10 The questions now are to what new age - or equal range of ages - the state scheme should move; and how quickly. As employers, occupational pension schemes and, of course, working people themselves will need to plan ahead, it will clearly be essential to give a reasonable period of notice of whatever change is decided upon, so that plans can be adjusted.

8.11 The information set out in this discussion paper is intended as background to help inform public debate on this important issue. Comments would be welcome and should be sent to:

> The Department of Social Security
> Room 1121A
> The Adelphi
> 1-11 John Adam Street
> London
> WC2N 6HT

by 30th June 1992. Please clearly mark correspondence 'State Pension Age Discussion Paper'.

Glossary

Activity rate:

The proportion of people in a given age group who are economically active, i.e. either working or seeking work.

Actuarially neutral adjustments to pensions:

Adjustments whereby the annual payments for a pension drawn early are lower than would otherwise be the case to reflect the fact that it would be paid for more years. Conversely, annual payments for a pension drawn later are higher to reflect the fact that it would be paid for fewer years. This ensures pensions have the same value taken over the whole period of payment.

Basic pension:

The flat rate element of a category A state pension based on the number of qualifying years accrued during an individual's working life. To qualify for full category A basic pension contributions must have been paid for around 90% of working life.

Class 1 contributions:

Compulsory earnings related national insurance contributions paid by employed earners (i.e. employees) and their employers. *(See entries for Primary and Secondary contributions and lower and upper earnings limits).*

Class 2 contributions:

Compulsory national insurance contributions paid by self-employed people. Flat rate weekly amount.

Class 3 contributions:

Voluntary national insurance contributions paid in order to make up a contribution record *(see below)*. Flat rate weekly amount.

Contracted-out scheme:

An occupational pension scheme which undertakes to meet certain conditions and provides rights for those members who join it instead of remaining in SERPS. In return Primary and Secondary Class 1 national insurance contributions are paid at a lower rate.

Contracted Out Money Purchase Scheme (COMP):

An occupational pension scheme which is contracted out of SERPS by reference to the payment of a minimum level of contributions in respect of each member rather than by reference to provision of a guaranteed minimum pension. Benefits are determined on a money purchase basis, i.e. the fund accrued is used to provide the pension either by the scheme or an insurance policy or the purchase of an annuity contract.

Contracted Out Salary Related Scheme (COSR):

An occupational pension scheme contracted out of SERPS in which benefits are related to earnings, either final earnings or average earnings.

Contribution limits:

See entries for lower and upper earnings limits.

Contribution record:
The record of the amount of contributions paid by, or credited to, each individual during the course of their working life.

Contribution test scheme:
A pension scheme wherein entitlement to a pension is based on paying a specified number of contributions (or achieving a set number of qualifying years - *see below*) rather than on reaching a set age.

Contribution year:
A period running from 6 April in one year to 5 April in the next.

Contributory benefits:
Benefits which provide for a specific contingency - such as retirement or sickness - and entitlement to which is based on payment of a set level of national insurance contributions.

Deferral:
Putting off claiming a pension either to earn increments or to continue to receive another benefit such as invalidity benefit. At present pension claims can be deferred for up to five years.

Demography:
The science of population statistics.

Dependant:
A person such as a spouse or child in respect of whom an increase of basic benefit can be paid.

Earnings rule:
A provision which either prevented a person taking a pension because of earnings over the specified limit or reduced a pension once in payment. The rule was abolished in October 1989.

Economically active:
Either working or seeking work.

Equivalent Pension Benefit:
The minimum pension benefits which had to be provided by an occupational pension scheme which contracted-out of the graduated pension scheme.

European Council Directive:
An instruction to all Member States regarding the operation of a specified aspect of Community policy, e.g. equal treatment. Takes precedence over domestic legislation.

Graduated Pension Scheme:

The earnings related state scheme which commenced on 3 April 1961 and terminated on 5th April 1975.

Gross Domestic Product (GDP):

The total value of all goods and services produced domestically during a year.

Guaranteed Minimum Pension:

The minimum pension benefits which must be provided by a contracted-out salary-related scheme.

Home Responsibilities Protection:

A scheme which reduces the number of qualifying years necessary for a full pension for people who are unable to work because they have to stay at home to look after someone such as a child or sick relative.

Income-related benefits:

Benefits which are available to people with low incomes and which vary in the amount payable according to the income of the beneficiary. Not based on payment of national insurance contributions.

Income-related benefit expenditure:

The annual amount of public expenditure spent on providing income-related benefits.

Increments:

An addition to pension entitlement earned by deferment of claim. At present, increments of around 7.5% of the pension entitlement can be awarded for each year of deferral. Increments are not awarded where claims are deferred to continue receiving certain contributory benefits.

Lower Earnings Limit (LEL):

The level of earnings (weekly, monthly or annual) below which there is no liability to pay national insurance contributions.

National insurance contributions:

Payable by employers, employees, self-employed and voluntary contributors into the National Insurance Fund to support the payment of contributory benefits.

National Insurance Fund:

A pool of money financed by national insurance contributions and investment income from which the current cost of contributory benefits is met.

Net average income:

Weekly average income after deductions for income tax and national insurance contributions.

Non-contributory benefits:
> Benefits which provide for a specific contingency where entitlement is based on fulfilment of set qualifying conditions and not payment of national insurance contributions, e.g. attendance allowance, child benefit.

Occupational Pension Scheme:
> An arrangement organised by an employer or on behalf of a group of employers to provide pensions and/or other benefits for or in respect of one or more employees on leaving service or on death or retirement.

Pay-as-you-go:
> The operating nature of state pension provision whereby pensions in payment are funded by the current contributions of the present working population.

Personal Pensions:
> Pension contracts between individuals and pension providers such as insurance companies or financial institutions.

Primary Class 1 national insurance contributions:
> National insurance contributions paid by employees at a level depending on their earnings.

Principal projections:
> The main population projections for Great Britain prepared by the Government Actuary's Department.

Qualifying year:
> A tax year in which qualifying earnings of at least 52 times the weekly lower earnings limit for that year have been received or treated as received.

Retirement age:
> The age at which people stop work to retire. Can differ from pension age - *see entry for state pension age.*

Retirement Pension expenditure:
> The annual amount of public expenditure spent on providing state retirement pensions.

Secondary Class 1 national insurance contributions:
> National insurance contributions paid by employers as a percentage of their employees' earnings.

Single European market:
> Freedom of movement for goods, for services, for people and for capital throughout the Community.

Split retirement scheme:
A pension scheme wherein elements of the state pension (such as basic pension and SERPS) become payable at different ages.

State Earnings Related Pension (SERPS) Additional pension:
The earnings related element of state pension. Entitlement is calculated as a specified percentage of earnings since April 1978 on which national insurance contributions have been paid, revalued at pension age to take into account the increase in average earnings.

State pension age:
The earliest age at which state pension can be drawn.

Support ratio:
The number of people of working age per pensioner.

Upper Earnings Limit (UEL):
The level of earnings (weekly monthly or annual) above which there is no liability to pay primary Class 1 national insurance contributions. *(N.B. There is no upper earnings limit for secondary Class 1 national insurance contributions.)*

Uprating:
The increase in benefit rates normally announced each October.

Variable rate scheme:
A pension scheme wherein pension can be drawn at any age within a range around a 'pivotal age' at which the full pension is awarded. Pensions claimed before the pivotal age are paid at a reduced rate; pensions claimed after the pivotal age are paid at an enhanced rate.

Working age:
From minimum school leaving age to pension age. In the UK this is currently 16-59 for women and 16-64 for men.

Working life:
The number of years between minimum school leaving age and pension age. Currently 44 for women and 49 for men.

APPENDIX 1: THE FINANCIAL EFFECTS OF MOVING TO A COMMON STATE PENSION AGE

Introduction

1.   The need to examine the effects on public finances of equalising male and female state pension ages has long been recognised. The results presented in this appendix are the latest in a series of estimates.

2.   In 1982 a report from the Social Services Committee[1] looked at the possibility of equalising state pension age. In its evidence to that Committee, the then Department of Health and Social Security presented estimates of the effect on public finances of equalising state pension age. These figures, updated to 1985 prices have been, until now, the most up-to-date estimates available.

3.   This appendix presents new estimates of the effects on public finances of equalising the state pension age. These estimates cover equalisation at ages 60 and 65, the current state pension ages for women and men respectively, and age 63, which comes closest to providing a cost-neutral equalised state pension age.

4.   The new estimates differ from previous estimates in two ways :-

   i)   Previous estimates looked at the financial effects on the assumption that changes to state pension age had been made overnight. There are two disadvantages with this assumption. First, not allowing for a period of implementation is clearly unrealistic. Secondly, the cost of the state scheme will rise considerably over the first half of the next century as a result of the increased number of pensioners and the increase in the total amount of SERPS payable. The new estimates attempt to assess the financial effects over a time period that allows for a period of implementation and the rise in the cost of the state scheme. This means assessing the effects well into the future.

   ii)   The new estimates attempt to take into account a number of effects not included in previous estimates. In particular, they take account of how the labour market effects of changing state pension age will affect public finances.

5.   The new estimates are however subject to considerable uncertainty. There are obvious difficulties in predicting developments well into the future. Some of these are discussed further in *paragraphs 42-48* below. In modelling the labour market effects, a number of simplifications and assumptions have to be made. For these reasons, *the results should not be interpreted as precise estimates but as broad indicators of the financial effects.*

---

[1]Age of Retirement Third Report from the House Of Commons Social Services Committee, Session 1981-82, HMSO, (1982), HC 26.

Scope of the Estimates

Types of financial effects

6.   The estimates include two types of financial effect :-

   i)   **Direct financial effects** will occur automatically from the application of new rules governing entitlement to state retirement pension. For example, if male pension age is reduced to 60, men aged 60-64 will become entitled to state retirement pension and spending on state retirement pensions will rise.

   ii)   **Indirect financial effects** will occur because changing state pension age will affect people's behaviour. If male state pension age is reduced to 60, for example, a man who was planning to retire at age 65 may now decide to retire at 60, especially if the normal retirement age in his occupational pension scheme were changed. He may also revise his own savings plans to allow for this earlier than anticipated retirement. There will therefore be other financial effects as people, companies and other institutions adjust to the changes in state pension age and these adjustments work their way through the economy. For example, a change in state pension age may cause some men to retire earlier than originally planned. If some of the jobs that they vacate are taken by people who would otherwise have been unemployed, then there would be a saving in unemployment benefit expenditure.

7.   The 1982 estimates included some indirect effects. For instance, the estimates allowed for the likelihood outlined above that a number of the jobs vacated by newly-entitled pensioners would be filled by the unemployed. The new estimates attempt to extend the 1982 methodology to include further indirect effects of changing state pension age.

8.   Although the new estimates represent an advance on previous estimates, they do not encompass all the conceivable effects on public finances of changing state pension age, e.g. no allowance has been made for effects on corporation tax. How people, companies and other institutions would respond to changes in state pension age and how these responses would affect the variables in the economy that in turn affect public finances are matters of some uncertainty. Attempting to quantify these effects is even more difficult.

9.   It should be emphasised that the estimates are concerned only with the effects on public finances of changing state pension age. There will of course be wider economic consequences. These are discussed further in *Chapter 6.*

The Time Period Covered by the Estimates

10. Estimates are presented for two dates : 2025 and 2035. This is because :

- the number of pensioners in the age group 60-64 is projected to peak around 2025. The year 2025 is therefore useful as an indicator of the maximum scale of the financial effects in the first half of the next century;

- after 2025, the number of people who would be affected drops away. By 2035 it is assumed to be reasonably stable. 2035 is therefore a reasonably representative indicator of the scale of the financial effects up to 2050.

11. The timing and speed of the implementation will obviously determine the timing of the financial effects of equalisation. This is discussed briefly in *Chapter 6*. For the purposes of assessing the financial implications over the period starting in 2025, it is assumed that the changes are fully in place in that year. Clearly the changes might be fully implemented some years before then.

Outline of the New Methodology

12. Equalising state pension ages at 60, 63 or 65, may be broken down into two steps : the reduction, if any, in the male state pension age; and the increase, if any, in the female state pension age.

13. The financial effects resulting from each of these adjustments are assessed separately, using analogous calculations. These are then added to give the overall financial effects. This task is obviously simplified for ages 60 and 65, where only one pension age is changed so these examples are used to illustrate the approach.

14. The direct and indirect effects of equalising pension ages discussed above may each be broken down into a further two main categories. These are described below. *Appendix 3* provides a detailed breakdown of these elements.

Direct Effects on State Retirement Pension

15. If state pension age is equalised at 60, men aged between 60 and 64 will become entitled to state retirement pension and total expenditure on state retirement pensions will rise. If state pension age is equalised at 65, women between 60 and 64 will no longer be entitled to state retirement pension and total expenditure on state retirement pensions will be reduced. The size of these changes in expenditure will depend on the numbers affected by the change in pension entitlements and their average entitlement to state retirement pension. Long term projections of these factors are necessarily subject to some uncertainty *(see paragraphs 42-48)*. The detailed assumptions regarding these two factors are set out in *Appendix 3*.

Other Direct Effects of Changes in Entitlement to State Retirement Pension

16. The changes in people's entitlements to state retirement pension will lead to a number of direct effects on their entitlement to other benefits and their liability to income tax :-

i) **Income tax** - state retirement pension counts as part of a person's taxable income. If state pension age is equalised at age 60, any consequent income tax collected will partly offset increased retirement pension expenditure. Conversely, some of the saving in state retirement pension created by removing entitlement from women aged 60-64, if equalising at age 65, will be offset by the fall in the income tax collected from these women.

ii) **Contributory benefits** - if male state pension age is reduced, some of the men becoming entitled to state retirement pension would otherwise have been receiving other contributory benefits, such as invalidity benefit and spending on these benefits will fall. Increasing female state pension age has the converse effect.

iii) **Income-related benefits** - if state pension age is equalised at age 60, some of the men who will become entitled to state retirement pension would otherwise have been receiving income-related benefits. The increase in these men's assessable income will reduce their entitlements to these benefits and spending on income-related benefits will be reduced. Conversely, equalising state pension age at age 65 will reduce the assessable income of those women aged 60-64 receiving income-related benefits by removing their entitlement to state retirement pension. Consequently, expenditure on income-related benefits will rise.

17. These effects arise from the direct application of the rules governing benefit entitlements and liability to income tax; they do not rely on any changes in the behaviour of those people affected by the changes to state pension age. These effects act on the Exchequer in the opposite direction to the initial effects caused by the changes in state retirement pension entitlements. These effects will sometimes be referred to as the *'other'* direct effects as opposed to the *'state retirement pension'* direct effects.

Financial Effects Resulting from the Impact of Changes to State Pension Age on the Labour Market

18. If male pension age is reduced to 60 some men will retire earlier. This will reduce the number of men who are either working or actively seeking work. Raising female state pension age will defer some women's retirement and increase the number of women who are working or actively seeking work.

19. These changes in the supply of labour will affect the average level of wages and salaries, the numbers of people in employment, and the numbers of people in unemployment. The resulting changes in aggregate wages and salaries in the economy will affect receipts of income tax and national insurance contributions. Unemployment benefit expenditure will change as a result of the impact on the level of unemployment. These effects are spelt out in more detail in *Appendix 3.*

Effect of State Pension Age Limit on Employees' National Insurance Contributions

20. At present, people working on past state pension age do not have to pay Class 1 primary national insurance contributions. It is assumed that this alignment would continue following any changes to male and female state pension ages. If state pension age is equalised at 60, no employee contributions would be collected from those men who continue to work between the ages of 60 and 64. If state pension age is equalised at 65, employee contributions will be payable by those women who work on between the ages of 60 and 64. For brevity, this will sometimes be referred to as the *'age limit'* effect on contributions.

21. The number of people working on past state pension age will depend on how people react to changes to state pension age. This is also an indirect effect. The assumptions that are made in calculating this effect are set out in *Appendix 3.*

Main Assumptions

22. To calculate the above effects a number of assumptions have to be made about any tax and benefits policy changes and economic and demographic developments that might be expected between now and 2025.

23. It is assumed that present policy in relation to benefits and contributions will continue. In particular, it is assumed that benefit entitlements and the contributory system will be modified only by making entitlement conditions and liability to pay national insurance contributions move into line with the specified change to state pension age. No account is taken of any changes that might be made to finance the Exchequer costs or savings. These are discussed further in *Chapter 6*.

24.   The central uprating assumption is that all benefits are uprated and contribution limits re-rated in line with prices. *Appendix 2* sets out the results of making the alternative assumption that all benefits and limits are uprated in line with earnings except for additional pensions in payment, which are uprated in line with prices.

25.   It is assumed that real earnings grow by 1.5% per annum as assumed in the Government Actuary's 2nd Quinquennial Review[1] and in the 1985 Green Paper[2]. This is below the actual average rate of growth in real earnings in the post-war period of about 2 per cent. An alternative set of estimates has been produced on a higher earnings growth assumption of 2.25% per annum. The results are set out in *Appendix 2*.

What the Estimates Show

26.   The following paragraphs examine three aspects of the implications for public finances of equalising state pension age.

---

[1] National Insurance Fund Long Term Financial Estimates; Report by the Government Actuary on the Second Quinquennial Review under section 137 of the Social Security Act 1975; July 1990

[2] Reform of Social Security; June 1985; Cmnd 9517-9

Overall Impact on Public Finances

27. Changing state pension age will affect spending on state retirement pension, other contributory benefits and the income-related benefits. Government revenues from income tax and national insurance contributions will also be affected. Adding together all of these effects produces an estimate of the overall net impact on the Exchequer. *Figure 1* below summarises the main estimates of the impact on the Exchequer in 2025 and 2035. These estimates are based on assumptions which are subject to some uncertainty. *(See paragraphs 42-48).*

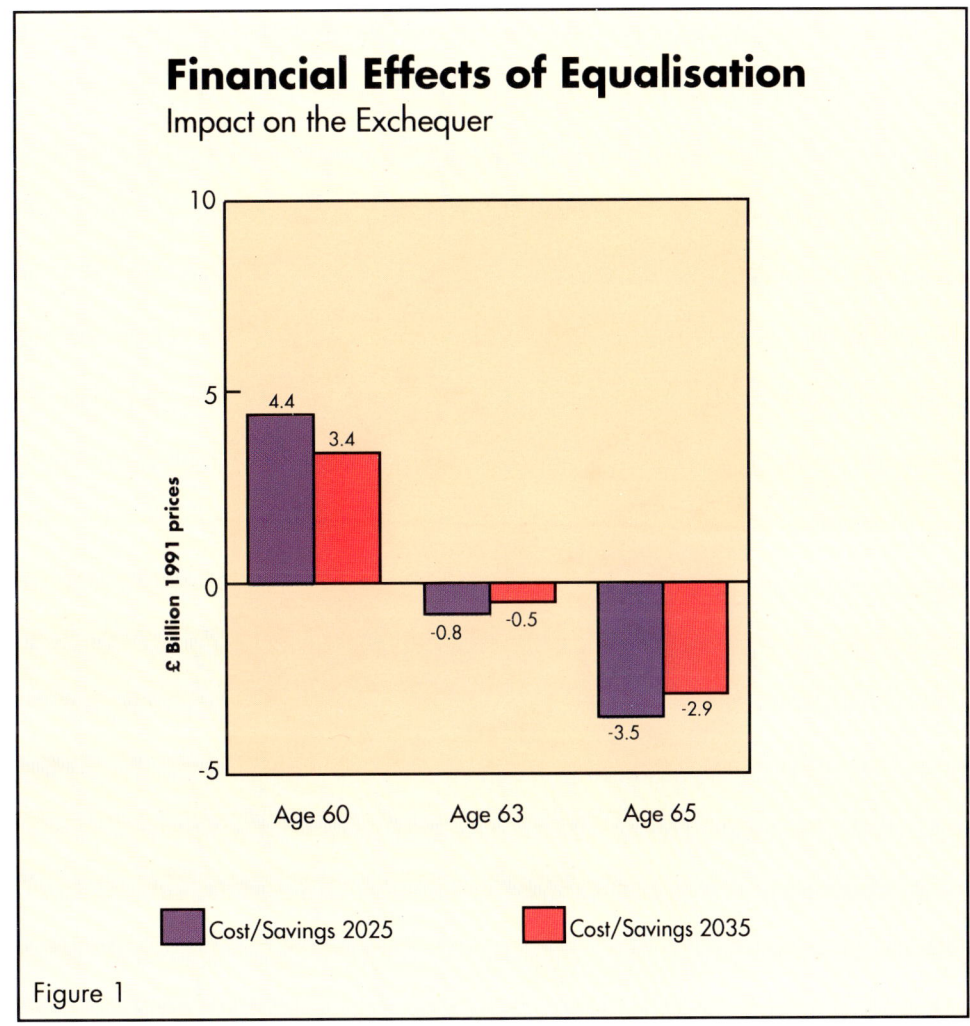

Financial Effects of Equalisation
Impact on the Exchequer

Figure 1

Composition of the Exchequer Costs and Savings

28.   **Equalisation at age 60** - as might be expected, extending entitlement to state retirement pension to a large number of men produces a substantial increase in state retirement pension expenditure of around £6.9 bn for a prices uprating. *Figure 2* shows the composition of the impact on the Exchequer in 2035 for equalisation at age 60. The other direct effects yield a saving of £3.2 bn. The labour market effects yield a saving of £0.9 bn that slightly outweighs the £0.7 bn cost produced by the national insurance contributions age limit effect. The net impact on the Exchequer amounts to a cost of around £3.4 bn.

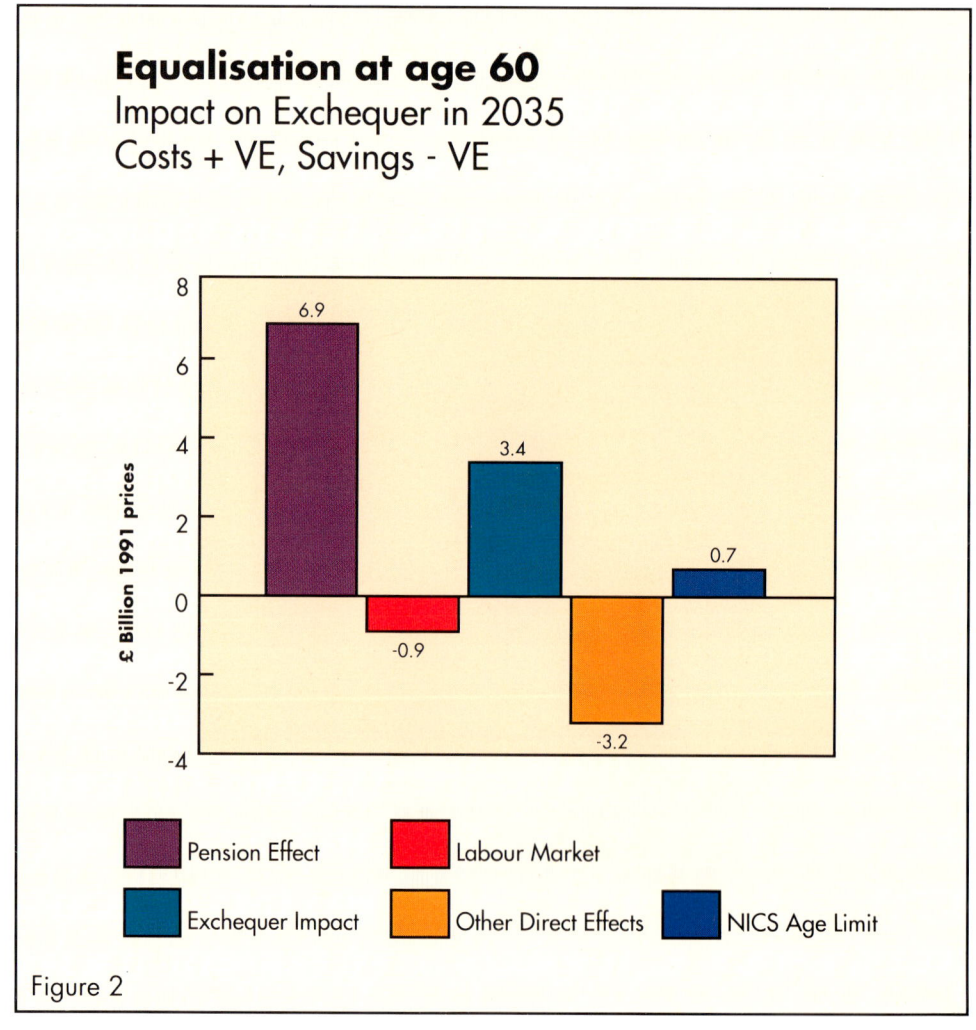

Figure 2

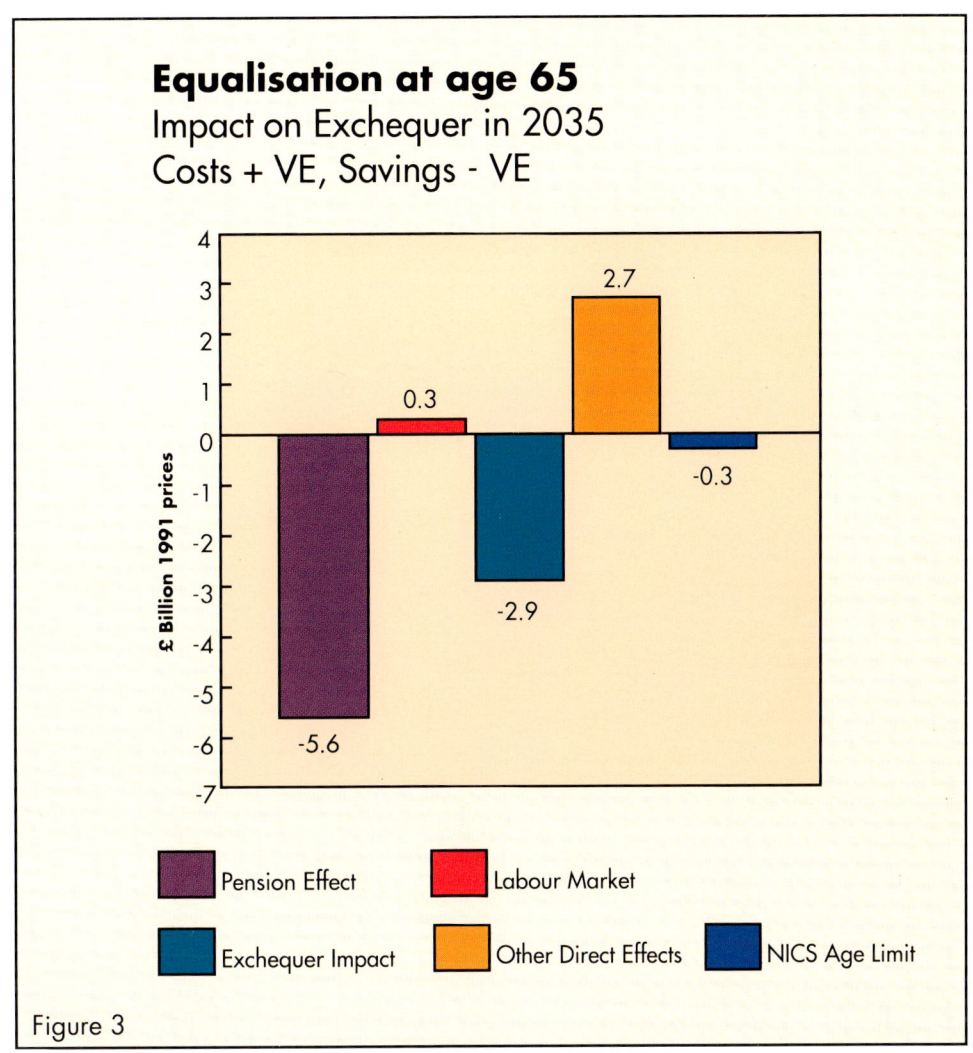

Equalisation at age 65
Impact on Exchequer in 2035
Costs + VE, Savings - VE

£ Billion 1991 prices

- Pension Effect
- Labour Market
- Exchequer Impact
- Other Direct Effects
- NICS Age Limit

Figure 3

29. **Equalisation at age 65** - removing entitlement to state retirement pension from a large number of women produces a substantial saving of around £5.6 bn. *Figure 3* shows the composition of the impact on the Exchequer in 2035 for equalisation at age 65. The other direct effects amount to a cost of about £2.7 bn. As for age 60, the labour market effect and the age limit effect on contributions tend to cancel each other out. Finally, the net impact on the Exchequer is a saving of around £2.9 bn.

30. **Equalisation at age 63** - the effect of removing entitlement to state retirement pension from women aged 60-62 outweighs the effect of extending entitlement to men aged 63-64 to produce a saving of around 0.3 bn. *Figure 4* shows the composition of the impact on the Exchequer in 2035 for equalisation at age 63. The other effects are fairly small, because the male and female effects cancel each other out. The net impact on the Exchequer is a saving of around £0.5 bn.

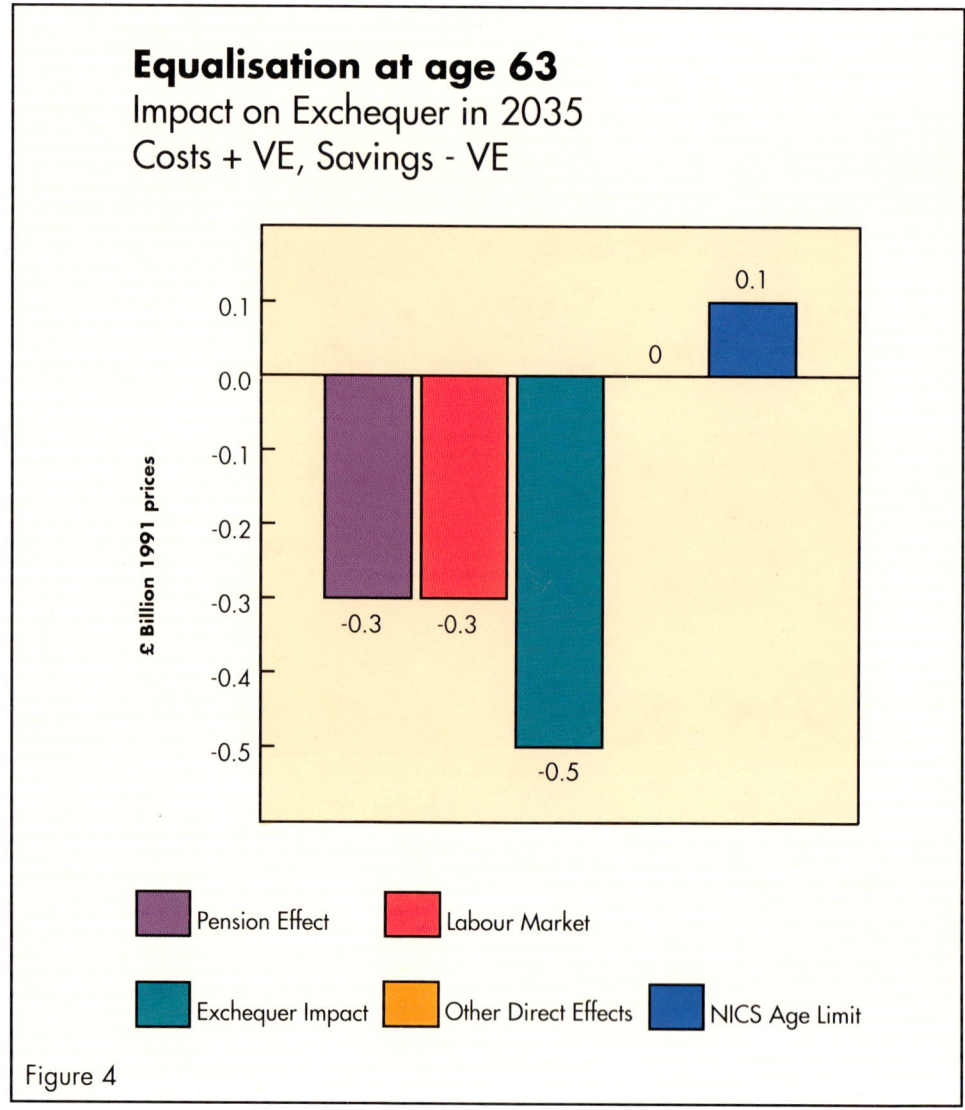

Figure 4

31. The overall conclusions to be drawn from these graphs are that :

- the effect on the Exchequer of expenditure on state retirement pension by far outweighs the other effects;

- consequently, whatever reasonable alternative assumptions are adopted for assessing the other effects, equalisation at age 60 will carry a considerable cost and equalisation at age 65 will produce a considerable saving;

- at some age between 60 and 65 there will be a cost-neutral point. This is close to age 63.

Effect on Public Expenditure

32. Changes in the overall level of public expenditure are an important measure of the scale of public involvement in the economy, as are other indicators, such as public expenditure as a proportion of national income, which are derived from it. Estimates have been made of the impact that changing state pension age would have on public expenditure by adding together all of the effects on contributory and income-related benefits. These estimates are summarised in *Figure 5*.

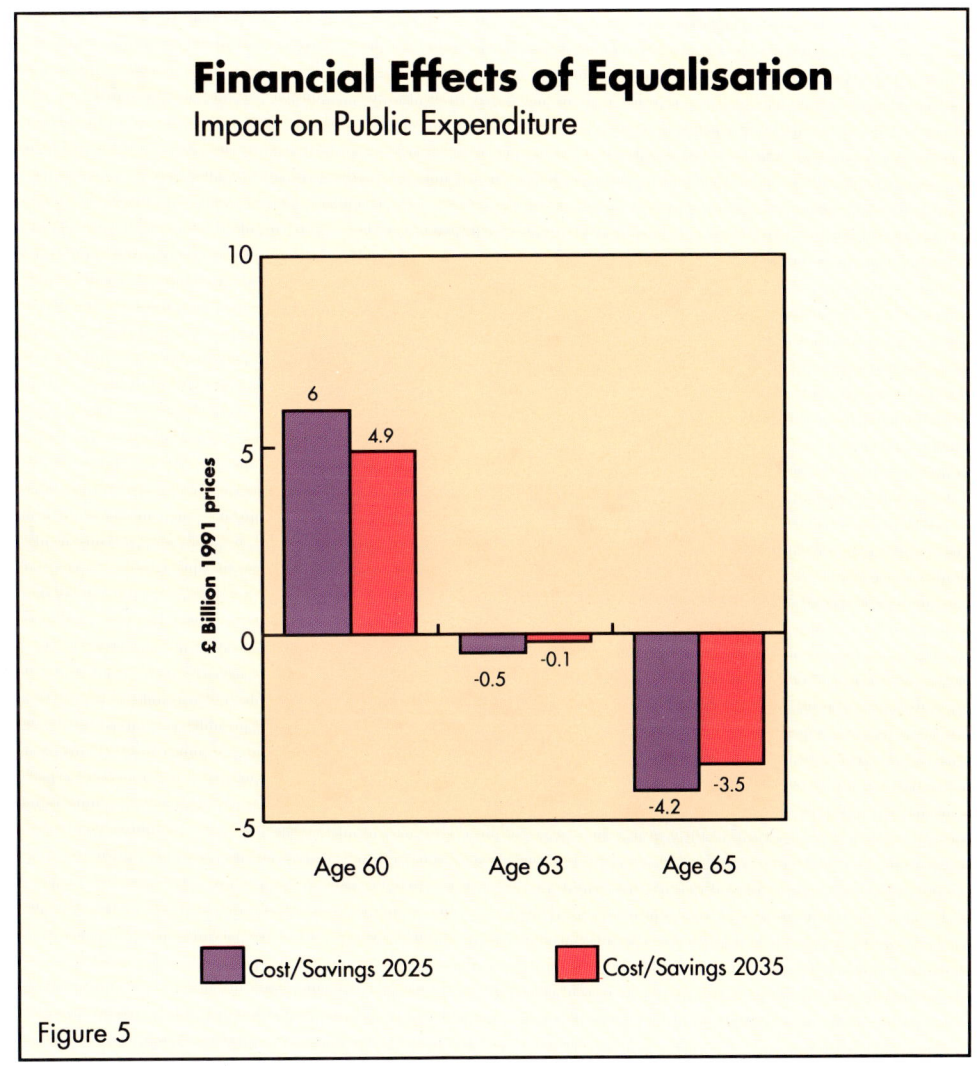

Financial Effects of Equalisation
Impact on Public Expenditure

Figure 5

Effect on the National Insurance Fund

33. State retirement pension is the principal contributory benefit and is financed through the National Insurance Fund. The Fund is operated on a pay-as-you-go basis, i.e. the rates of national insurance contributions payable are set at a level intended to produce a flow of income that will broadly match expenditure on the contributory benefits and administration costs. Changing state pension age will affect both the overall level of spending on contributory benefits paid out of the Fund and the level of contributions paid into it. Estimates have been made both of the net impact on the Fund and of the possible adjustments to contribution rates that would be required to restore its balance. *Figure 6* below sets out the estimates of the effects on the National Insurance Fund.

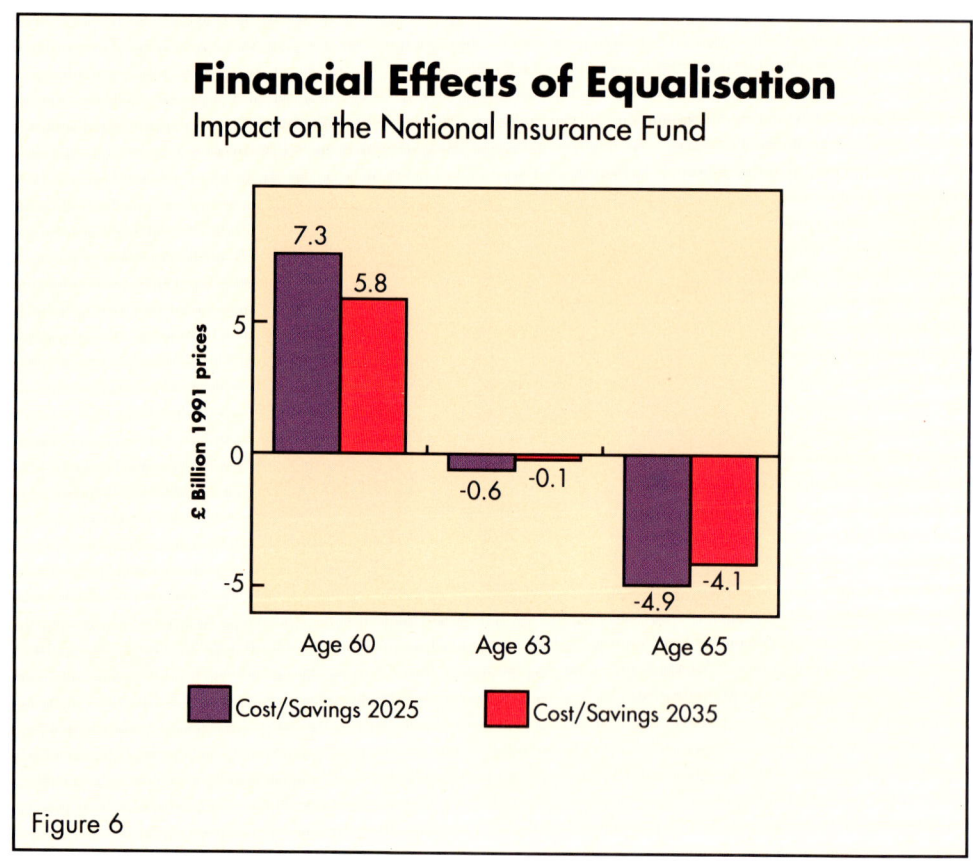

Figure 6

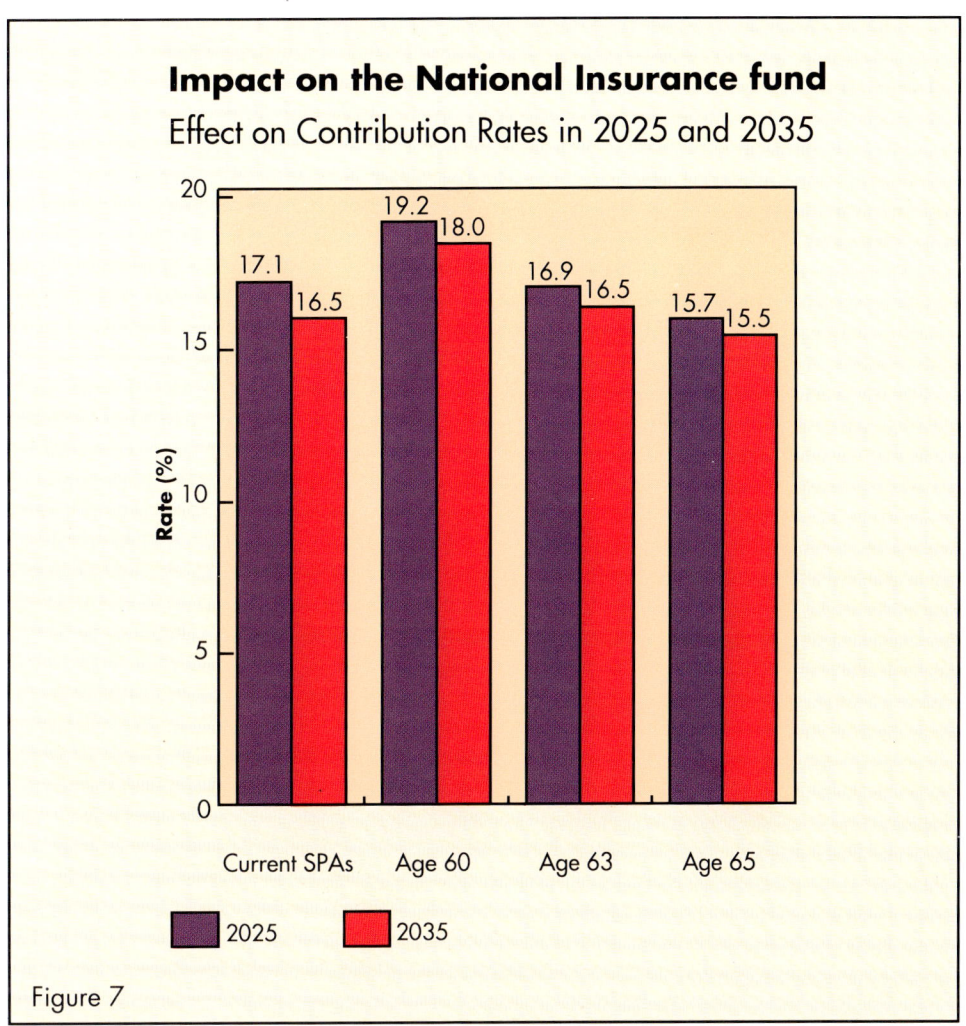

Impact on the National Insurance fund

Effect on Contribution Rates in 2025 and 2035

Figure 7

34. *Figure 7* above shows the projected contribution rates that would be required in 2025 and 2035 to balance the National Insurance Fund assuming firstly no change to state pension age and then allowing for the effects on the Fund of equalisation at age 60, 63 and 65. These changes in contribution rates would bring the Fund back into balance. The increase or decrease in the level of national insurance contributions would, however, overcompensate for the costs or savings to the Exchequer. This is because the impact of changing state pension age on the National Insurance Fund is always greater than the overall effect on the Exchequer. This is explained in *paragraphs 36-40.*

Summary of Results

35. These figures show that :-

    i)   **Equalisation at age 60**
The National Insurance Fund would be unbalanced to the extent of £7.3 bn in 2025 and £5.8 bn in 2035. This would require combined employer and employee Class 1 contribution rates to be 2 percentage points higher than otherwise in 2025 and 1.5 percentage points higher in 2035.

    ii)   **Equalisation at age 63**
The National Insurance Fund would show a very slight favourable effect in 2025 of £0.6 bn and a small improvement in 2035 of £0.1 bn. This would allow combined employer and employee Class 1 contribution rates to be lower than otherwise by around 0.2 percentage points in 2025. The effect on contribution rates in 2035 would be minimal.

    iii)   **Equalisation at age 65**
The National Insurance Fund would show large favourable effects of £4.9 bn in 2025 and £4.1 bn in 2035. This would allow combined employer and employee Class 1 contribution rates to be 1.5 percentage points lower than otherwise in 2025 and 1 percentage point lower in 2035.

Relationship Between Measures of Financial Effects

36. Comparison of *Figures 2 to 4* shows that, for ages 60 and 65, there are significant differences in the absolute size of the three financial measures. The smallest is the effect on the Exchequer. The next largest is the effect on public expenditure. The effect on the National Insurance Fund is the greatest in absolute value. This relationship is explained below for equalisation at age 60 in 2025.

37. The effect on the Exchequer of a cost of £4.4 bn comprises four net effects:

- the net cost on contributory benefits of £6.9 bn;

- the net cost in national insurance contributions of £0.4 bn;

- the net savings in income-related benefits of 0.9 bn;

- the net savings in income tax of £2.0 bn.

38. To get from the Exchequer effect to the effect on public expenditure, the revenue effects have to be excluded. Since these amount to a net saving of £1.6 bn, i.e. the net saving in income tax of £2.0 bn less the net cost in national insurance contributions of £0.4 bn, the public expenditure effect is £1.6 bn larger in absolute size than the Exchequer effect at a cost of £6.0 bn.

39. To get the effect on the National Insurance Fund from the effect on public expenditure, the net cost in national insurance contributions of £0.4 bn must be added in and the saving of £0.9 bn in income-related benefits must be removed.

40. The same analysis applies to equalisation at age 65 but with the direction of the effects reversed. In both cases, the Exchequer effect is smallest in absolute magnitude with the public expenditure effect and the National Insurance Fund effects being successively larger. The situation is more complicated for age 63 because of the mixture of the effects of changing male and female pension ages and this relationship will not apply.

Effects Over Time

41.   As discussed above, 2025 represents a year in which the financial effects might be expected to peak and 2035 represents an indication of the longer term average once the pensioner population is more stable. *Figure 8* illustrates this pattern of the effects on the Exchequer over time.

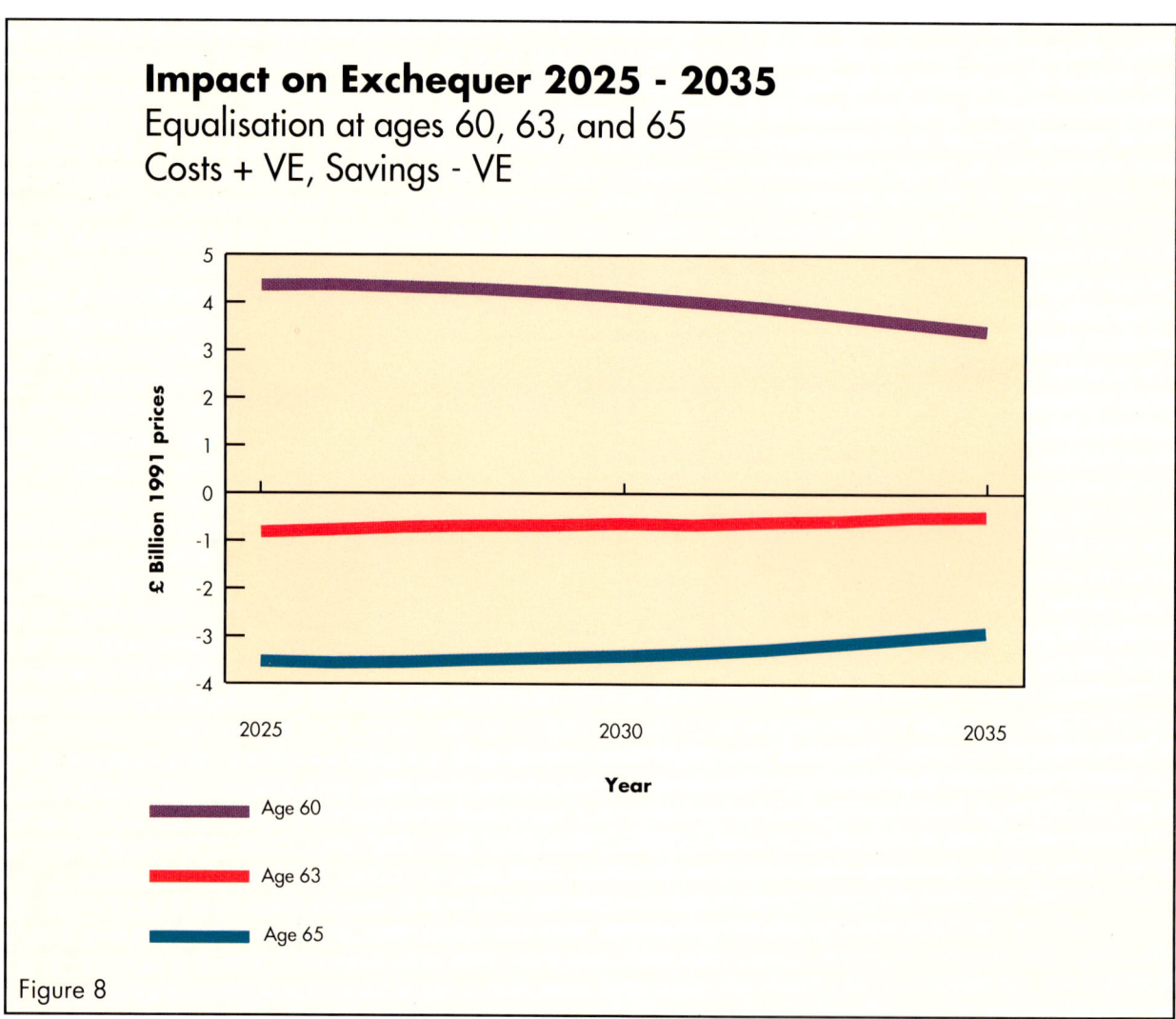

Impact on Exchequer 2025 - 2035
Equalisation at ages 60, 63, and 65
Costs + VE, Savings - VE

Age 60
Age 63
Age 65

Figure 8

Interpretation of the Estimates

42   Because these estimates look so far into the future, and make a large number of assumptions, they should obviously be treated as broad indicators rather than precise figures.

43.   It is also important to recognise that the assumptions that lead to these results differ in their robustness. This section discusses the nature of these assumptions and some implications for interpreting the estimates.

44. The assumptions made can be broadly categorised as follows:

- economic assumptions;

- demographic assumptions; and

- benefit caseload and level assumptions.

Economic Assumptions

45. Uncertainties associated with long term economic forecasting put these among the most debatable of all the assumptions underpinning the costings in this paper. Some analysis has therefore been done to assess how sensitive the central case estimates for 2035 are to variations in four key areas:

- elasticity of demand for labour;

- growth in pensioner incomes (excluding benefits);

- economic activity rates; and

- inflation.

Table 1 sets out the results of this analysis.

Demographic Assumptions

46. Assumptions in this area are reasonably robust. This is because the people who will be in the relevant age groups over the next 60 years are already alive. Some variation from these projections may nonetheless occur if mortality rates vary from the central projection.

Benefit Caseloads and Entitlements

47. Average benefit entitlements are by their very nature more difficult to predict. Assumptions about basic retirement pension average entitlements are reasonably robust and these are the main driving force behind the costings. Some other benefits are more difficult to forecast with confidence, such as activity rates, working patterns, contracting-out, take-up and other factors may change and interact. No attempt has been made to model potential variations in this area. In addition, no allowance has been made for potential policy change. *(See Appendix 3.)*

Conclusion

48. The combined effects of the uncertainties in all areas of the assumptions discussed above suggests that, while the estimates provide a reasonable indication of the order of magnitude of the financial effects, they do not provide a precise forecast of the financial consequences of equalisation.

Table 1: Results of Sensitivity Analysis (2035): Net impact on the Exchequer £ (Billions), Prices uprating			
Equalisation at:	Age 60	Age 63	Age 65
a) Central estimate	3.4	-0.5	-2.9
b) Elasticity of Demand =-0.5 for labour	1.4	-1.0	-2.3
c) Elasticity of Demand = -1 for labour	4.3	-0.2	-3.1
d) 3% real growth in Pensioner Income from savings and non-state pensions	3.5	-0.4	-3.0
e) 0% real growth in Pensioner Income from savings and non-state pensions	3.3	-0.6	-2.9
f) 50% Higher baseline activity rates	4.0	-0.3	-3.2
g) 50% Lower baseline activity rates	2.8	-0.6	-2.6
h) nominal rate of price inflation 2% higher	3.6	-0.4	-3.0
Combining Assumptions			
High baseline activity/ 3% pensioner income growth/ elasticity of demand = -1.0 [(c), (d) and (f) above]	5.4	+0.1	-3.4
Low baseline activity 0% pension Income growth/ elasticity of demand = -0.5 [(b), (e) and (g) above]	1.6	-0.9	-2.3
Costs + ve, (Savings -ve)			

APPENDIX 2: IMPACT ON THE FINANCIAL EFFECTS OF
i) EARNINGS UPRATINGS AND
ii) HIGHER EARNINGS GROWTH

This appendix compares the effects of assuming earnings upratings of benefits with the central assumption of prices upratings which is in line with current legislation. It also looks at the effect on both of these estimates of assuming higher earnings growth.

Effects of Alternative Uprating Assumption

1.   *Table 1* below compares the main results obtained under the prices uprating assumption and the earnings uprating assumption for the impact on the Exchequer in 2035. It shows quite clearly how the effect of moving to an earnings uprating assumption scales up the financial effect. This is because benefit rates are considerably higher under this assumption and so the costs and savings are magnified.

Table 1: Financial effects under alternative uprating assumptions (£ Billions 1991 Prices)		
SPA Equalised At Age -	**Prices Uprating**	**Earnings Uprating**
60	3.4	6.3
63	(–0.5)	(–0.8)
65	(–2.9)	(–5.2)
Costs + ve, (Savings -ve)		

Effects of Assuming Higher Earnings Growth

2.   The main estimates assume that real earnings grow on average by 1.5%. *Table 2* below compares the results obtained under this assumption with a higher rate of growth of 2.25% per annum. These results are again shown for the impact on the Exchequer in 2035.

Table 2: Financial effects under alternative uprating assumptions with prices uprating (£ Billions 1991 Prices)		
SPA Equalised At Age -	**Earnings Growth 1.5% P.A.**	**Earnings Growth 2.25% P.A.**
60	3.4	3.5
63	(–0.5)	(–0.6)
65	(–2.9)	(–3.0)
Costs + ve, (Savings -ve)		

3. *Table 2* shows that assuming higher earnings growth has little impact on the results. This is because the rate of growth of earnings does not substantially alter the key element of the estimates which is the effect on state retirement pension. Since the most important component of this - basic retirement pension - is uprated by prices and is therefore independent of the movement in earnings, assuming higher earnings growth has little effect.

4. This conclusion does not apply when benefit rates are determined by movements in earnings. *Table 3* below shows the results of assuming higher earnings growth under earnings uprating, again these are shown for the impact on the Exchequer in 2035.

Table 3: Financial effects under alternative earnings assumptions with earnings uprating (£ Billion, 1991 Prices)		
SPA Equalised At Age	**Earnings Growth 1.5% P.A.**	**Earnings Growth 2.25% P.A.**
60	6.3	9.6
63	(–0.8)	(–0.5)
65	(–5.2)	(–7.3)
Costs + ve, (Savings -ve)		

5. These results show that for earnings uprating, as might be expected, the financial impact would be magnified by the effect of a higher earnings assumption on benefit rates and hence on spending on state retirement pension - the most important component of the estimates. Given the long term relationship between earnings growth and economic growth, it should also be borne in mind that the third column in *Table 2* represents much smaller expenditure as a proportion of GDP than the second column, just as the second and third columns in *Table 3* could represent very similar levels of expenditure as a proportion of GDP.

APPENDIX 3: TECHNICAL DETAILS

1. This appendix describes in detail the method and assumptions used to produce the new estimates of the effect on public finances of equalising state pension age.

2. The estimates of the direct effects on public finances are crucially dependent on the number of people likely to be affected by any change in state pension ages and their entitlement to state retirement pension. Changes in state retirement pension entitlements will also have consequences for direct tax receipts and social security benefit expenditure.

3. The estimates of the indirect effects on public finances will also depend on the number of people who are affected by any change in state pension ages. As these indirect effects consist of those that result from changes in retirement patterns and the subsequent effects in the labour market, it is not only the absolute numbers of people affected that is important but also the proportion of economically active people who would be affected.

4. Two central components of the estimates are therefore the number of people aged 60-64 at the time of the change and the proportion of these people who are working, or seeking work, that is, their activity rates.

Number of People Likely to be Affected by Change in State Pension Age: Population Aged 60-64

5. Anybody who will be affected by these changes in the first half of the 21st Century has already been born. Unless there are unexpected developments in longevity or changes in net migration patterns, it is possible to forecast reliably the number of people in the key age groups at any one time. The post-war and 1960's baby booms are the key demographic influences affecting the number of potential new pensioners in the next half century. Post-war baby boomers are going to be retiring around the turn of the century and 1960's baby boomers are going to be retiring in the third and fourth decades of the 21st Century. Assuming any new state pension age is phased in slowly, the post-war baby boom will have little effect and the main demographic influence will be the 1960's baby boom. The approach to retirement of people born in the 1960s dominates the pattern of costs which peak around 2025. The decline from 2025 is eventually followed by further fluctuations as the children of the post-war and 1960's baby boomers gradually reach retirement age.

Activity Rates

6. The proportion of people working, or seeking work, in each age group is based on the forecast for the year 2001 by the Department of Employment in the May 1991 edition of the Employment Gazette. This neutral assumption has been used because the direction and scale of future trends in retirement decisions are not known with any precision and so it would be inappropriate to assume any particular trend. In recent years there has been an increasing tendency for men to retire earlier than previously and for women to retire slightly later than was formerly the case. These changes result from the influences of a number of variables including pensioners' wealth, potential incomes in and out of work, technical change making older workers' skills less relevant, and changing preferences for work and leisure. Whilst it is reasonable to presume that pensioners' wealth and income in retirement will continue increasing in the foreseeable future, changes in the other factors are much more difficult to estimate and the net effect on retirement patterns is a matter for considerable speculation. A range of alternative assumptions has been used to examine how sensitive the estimates are to different activity rates and the results of this work have been fed into the construction of the ranges set out in *Table 1* of *Appendix 1*.

Policy Assumptions, Timing and Financial Effects

7. Present policies with respect to entitlements or liabilities to all benefits and taxes are assumed to continue throughout. Changes are assumed to be in place by 2025. The components of the overall financial effects are explained in more detail below. The discussion is generally illustrated by reference to lowering male pension age to 60. Except where stated, raising female state pension age would have the same effects but in the opposite direction.

Direct Effects on Public Finances

Basic Retirement Pension

8. The estimates of the effect of changing state pension age on basic state retirement pension are based principally on assumptions about the future population and their benefit entitlement. On entitlement it is assumed that, for each cohort of people reaching pension age in the future, entitlement is as assumed in the Government Actuary's Quinquennial Review. The average rate of basic retirement pension is assumed to be unchanged for the new pension age.

9. The change in expenditure on basic retirement pension is then equal to the number of people newly entitled multiplied by the average annual rate of basic retirement pension. An allowance of 5% is made for pension payable overseas, in line with current trends.

SERPS

10. The underlying population and entitlement assumptions, including the effects of contracting-out, are based on the Government Actuary's

Quinquennial Review. Allowance is made for changes to the number of qualifying years giving entitlement as well as the different accrual rate at the new pension ages for each cohort.

Invalidity Benefit

11. Following a reduction in male state pension age, men below the current state pension age receiving invalidity benefit under the present rules would receive state retirement pension instead. There would consequently be an offsetting invalidity benefit saving to set against the increase in state retirement pension spending. This saving is based on the projected proportions of men and women assumed to be entitled to invalidity benefit. For men, this was assumed to be 16% at 60 rising to 22% at 64. For women, these proportions were extrapolated from present trends at ages up to 59, allowing for the impact of the phasing out of the married women's option on entitlement, giving an assumption of 8% at 60 rising to 10% at 64.

Widows' Benefit

12. This effect only arises when female state pension age is raised. Most widows no longer receiving state retirement pension at the ages affected are assumed to receive widows' benefit instead. This is assumed to be, on average, some 75% of the state retirement pension entitlement - based on the analysis in the Quinquennial Review of the long-term effect of the revisions to widows' benefit which came into force in 1988.

Adult Dependency Offset

13. If female state pension age is raised, the husbands of married women who are no longer receiving state retirement pension could become entitled to an adult dependency addition based on the husbands' entitlements to state retirement pension or other benefits such as invalidity benefit. The estimated offset is based on an analysis of the distribution of the ages of such husbands, the proportion entitled to benefit, and trends in the proportion entitled to dependency addition at ages up to 60 at present. For changes to male pension age, the effect on dependency additions is included with the benefit concerned.

Other Contributory Benefits

14. These effects are analogous to the effect on invalidity benefit but smaller. The financial effect is in the same proportion to the effect on invalidity benefit as current spending on these benefits is to current spending on invalidity benefit.

Income Tax Effect

15. Following a reduction in male state pension age, men aged 60 to 64 will be entitled to basic state retirement pension and SERPS. Since state retirement pension is taxable income, this will give rise to an offsetting increase in income tax revenue. Estimates of the scale of these effects are derived from the Department of Social Security's Policy Simulation Model [PSM][1], separately for men and women. These estimates are adjusted to allow for changes in the average value of people's marginal tax rates over time as the real value of incomes from private sources rises. It is assumed that pensioners' taxable non-benefit income (i.e. investment income, occupational and personal pensions, earnings, etc.) grows at 1.5% per annum in real terms.

Income Support Effect

16. If the male state pension age is reduced to 60, some income support claimants will find that their assessable income has risen by the amount of any receipt of state retirement pension or dependency addition. They will then lose some or all of their income support entitlement. Estimates at current levels of the scale of these effects are derived from the PSM. These are then adjusted to allow for changes in income support entitlement over time as the real value of incomes from private sources rises. A factor of 1.5% per annum has been used to reduce average income support payments over time to reflect the real growth in these income sources. By 2030 a fall of around 45% is applied to the basic PSM figures.

Housing Benefit Effect

17. This effect is analogous to the income support effect and is also derived from the DSS PSM. The effects are not however reduced over time: it is assumed that the growth in average housing costs will match the assumed growth in earnings, leaving the average housing benefit entitlement unchanged.

Other Effects

18. The above effects constitute the direct effects of changing state pension age. There will be further indirect effects as the changes in economic activity rates feed into the labour market. A reduction in the male state pension age, for example, will create vacancies as some men retire earlier than they would have done at the old state pension age. It has been assumed that three-quarters of these vacancies would be filled by the claimant unemployed and 25% from the increased economic activity of other people in the economy.

---

[1] The Policy Simulation Model is a detailed model of the income tax benefits system based on information from the Family Expenditure Survey.

19. There will also be further knock-on effects : the fall in labour supply will lead to increased real wages which in turn will reduce the total number of people in employment. The estimates of the effects on real wage rates and employment are based on estimates of the long run elasticities of demand and supply of labour taken from C.V. Brown et al, (1982/1983) 'Direct Taxation and Short Run Labour Supply' and 'Relationship between Employment and Wages: Empirical Evidence for the United Kingdom' H.M. Treasury, 1985.

20. The financial effects arising from these changes in the labour market are set out below.

Indirect Effects on Public Finances

Unemployment Benefit
Income Support
Housing Benefit

21. The effects on unemployment benefit, income support, and housing benefit are given by the change in unemployment multiplied by estimates of the proportions receiving the various benefits and the average amount received. These are derived from the PSM as for the state retirement pension effects on the income-related benefits. As for the state retirement pension effect, the income support figures are then adjusted to allow for changes in income support entitlement over time as the real value of incomes from private sources rises. Unemployment benefit and housing benefit figures are not adjusted.

Income Tax (Wage bill effect)
National Insurance Contributions (Wage bill effect)

22. The changes in wages and employment will change aggregate earnings in the economy and hence the amount raised by national insurance contributions and income tax - assuming no change in the average contribution and tax rates. The average contribution allows for changes to the real level of the lower earnings limit and upper earnings limit on the assumption of 1.5% real earnings growth. The underlying future contribution rates on current rules were based on those in the Quinquennial Review, assuming that future changes to the total national insurance contributions rates would apply proportionately to employees and employers.

23. The original level of real wages is derived from the GB average earnings figure for adults in all occupations for men, women working full-time and women working part-time in 1990-91, uprated to the starting date of the phasing of the change to the pension age.

Effect of State Pension Age Limit on Employees' National Insurance Contributions

24. It is assumed that the alignment of state pension age with the age at which people no longer have to pay national insurance contributions continues. If state pension age is equalised at 60, less national insurance contributions will be collected from the earnings of those men working on between the ages of 60 and 64. If state pension age is equalised at 65, increased national insurance contributions will be payable in respect of women working on between the ages of 60 and 64. The numbers working on after changes to state pension age are derived from the population projections and activity rate assumptions discussed above.

Printed in the United Kingdom for HMSO
Dd. 0509606 12/91 C60 (6986) 51-1002